The Final Flight
Divine Revelations of the Return of Jesus

JOSHUA ADETUNJI

Published by RUWEMI Ministries (Joshua Adetunji)
Author: Joshua Adetunji
ISBN-10: 1717145221
ISBN-13: 978-1717145222

DEDICATION

To Jesus Christ, for His loving kindness towards me; for His sacrifice on Calvary cross and for His continued role as my chief intercessor. I love you Jesus. To the Holy Spirit who inspired the writing. And to God for His loving kindness towards me.

CONTENTS

Acknowledgments   1
A Note from the Author   3
Introduction   5
Chapter 1 – I Was Taken Up   11
Chapter 2 – The Final Flight-Bible   16
Chapter 3 – 2017-The Year of Jubilee   20
Chapter 4 – I Saw the Antichrist   27
Chapter 5 – Jesus and the Dead Rise   30
Chapter 6 – Are the Righteous Dead in Heaven?   36
Chapter 7 – Where Then Are the Righteous Dead   43
Now?
Chapter 8 – Is Paradise Adjacent to Hell?   52
Chapter 9 – Life Triangle – Holy Trinity Explained   64
Chapter 10 – The Second Heaven – Hades   70
Chapter 11 – Where Are the Sinful Dead?   77
Chapter 12 – A Comfort Medicine   85
Chapter 13- The Controversy   88
Chapter 14 – Unity and Readiness for the Flight   101
Chapter 15 – Protein Needed in Church   137
Chapter 16 – The Third Creation Event   155
Chapter 17 – The Last Revival   176
Chapter 18 – A Glorious Journey   180
Chapter 19 – A Call to Action   193
Epilogue   195

ACKNOWLEDGMENTS

My wife and children, my siblings, my mother and late father. My pastors and teachers at school. Friends who I have been fortunate to share my journey in life and ministry with. My colleagues and superiors at work. All the volunteers for the programs organized by RUWEMI Ministries. You have all contributed in one way or the other to my life's journey. Thank you all.

A Note from the Author

First of three books that Jesus directed me to write, I have attempted to tailor it for both believing and non-believing readers. For this reason, a few word choices were made to balance this need. First, the title, "The Final Flight" is used instead of the word "rapture", mostly used by believing Christians to describe the same event written in the scripture. The operative subtitle is styled "Divine Revelations of the Return of Jesus".

Indeed, many of the stories recounted in the book were divinely revealed in open visions, dream visions, the still small voice of the Holy Spirit, audible voice of God, inner witness. However, not all the content of this book are revelations.

Some are divine inspirations enabled by the Holy Spirit while I was writing. Sometimes it was Jesus Himself at the centre of my adventures. Other times it was an adventure enabled by the Holy Spirit. Still on one occasion, I heard the audible voice of God the Father.

The Father, the Son and the Holy Spirit are one. In one instance, instead of using the words "Yes sir" which was my actual spontaneous response to Jesus, I elected to instead replace this with the phrase "Yes Lord".

In the interest of non-believing readers of this book, I have elected to use the word "Jesus" for all three of the same Trinity God in many cases. I have also attempted to also tell of vivid encounters with the other side- the side of darkness. This book is by no means a perfect piece, having been written by an imperfect man.

But the stories, the encounters and those mentioned in the visions are perfectly and tangibly true. Moreover, I have made efforts to ensure that both the inspirations and the revelations line up with the written word in the scriptures.

I gave the manuscript to four different pastors who have a heart for the kingdom, for a substance preview.

Finally, upon the completion of my writing, I embarked on a fasting and prayer for the Lord to reveal to me if by any chance I have misrepresented or misunderstood what He intended for me to put in the book. The message, value and benefits of the book is better realized if read from the beginning to the end.

Finally, this book is a progressive release of the revelations Jesus will be providing on this subject, hence it may be republished later.

Joshua Adetunji

> *The world we live in was not built to last forever.*
> *There is a Kingdom of God that lasts for eternity.*

INTRODUCTION

When the Wright Brothers invented the first successful flying aircraft in 1903, there was a global culture and appetite for a flying object that would defy gravity because necessity called for it. European, American and French inventors already made aeronautic advances though with meagre success.

Those who were optimistic for an aviation success were generally engineers and science believers. They were those who believed that the unchanging law of gravity would not allow any object suspended in the air– whatever goes up must surely come down.

But they felt the need to overcome the obstacle. With persistence, gravity was overcome. And the first successful aircraft flight carrying people was achieved. There were skeptics among European aviation inventors and newspapers who criticized the brothers.

In their criticism is found traces of unbelief that a successful flying machine could ever be sustained because of repeated disappointments. The Wright brothers endured all with their conviction for a breakthrough that has become part of the normal aspect of our everyday life.

It is unknown whether the brothers, sons of a preacher, were inspired by the bible that contains several instances where gravity was defied.

One of bible's most important subjects.

My focus in this book is to spotlight what should be considered one of bible's most important doctrines – the final flight of the believers of Jesus from this world into their eternal home in the Kingdom of God with Jesus leading the way.

I will explain why it's one of bible's most important subjects later. The experience with aviation invention described above is like what we can see today regarding the final flight, which is a bible doctrine described as the rapture by believing Christians.

The aviation skeptics of the eighteen hundred were generally believers in science and engineering. But the power of science and engineering was not enough to convince them that a successful flying machine can be built and sustained.

Sadly, in the same way, many believers of Jesus today are either not taught on this important subject or they have ceased talking about it because it is controversial as some claim, or they ceased believing in it because it has taken long for the Lord Jesus to come.

Some even contend that the followers of Jesus in the early church of the bible thought Jesus would return in their lifetime. As Jesus did not come, these early believers may have waited in vain.

I have interacted with many believers who believe that Jesus will come someday but they do not feel the need to expect Him or they do not believe Jesus would come in their lifetime. Others are very reluctant to even be seen to be associated with the doctrine of the rapture, or as I describe in this book, the final flight of the saints.

But the Lord Jesus gave me very important revelatory knowledge on this subject to share with you as His return is much more imminent than we have ever imagined. The intent of this is to get you ready, excited, hopeful and

The Son knew the season, the year

expectant of this unshakable hope for everyone who believes in Jesus.

Let's go back again to the days of the Wright Brothers. As I mentioned above, much discussions, gossips, skepticism, and opinions about the prospect of a successful flying machine resided mainly with believers in science, engineering and aviation and the press that gave them a voice.

There is little to no suggestion that the general public were carried along in this prospect or were aware or concerned for it. In the same way, today, this subject of the final flight of Jesus' believers is generally unknown, or not understood or appreciated among those who do not believe in Jesus.

The second intent of this book is then to spotlight to the rest of the world that the long held biblical belief of the Christian hope will soon materialize and the final flight of Christians from this world will happen any minute from now. Jesus said no one knows, not even Jesus Himself, knows the day or the hour when He will return to the earth except God in heaven (Mathew 24:36).

But notice that Jesus says no one knows the "day" or the "hour". At the time He made this declaration on earth, Jesus was very much familiar with other time metrics or indicators, for examples, "season", "month", "week" year. In a different context, Jesus affirmed that every word He spoke came directly from His Father God in heaven.

So, it was God speaking to Jesus at the point He made this statement regarding the time of His return. The Son perhaps knew the season, the year, the month and the week, except for the day or the hour.

Hence in the same context, He gave clues, signs that we should watch for that point to the beginning of the end of the world. An end that starts with His return.

As that scripture says, the day will come like a thief in the night with many caught by surprise. Jesus did not want the day to come as a surprise to His faithful followers, hence He gave the signs.

Today, we see the signs of the last days in increasing proportion and intensity. The extent of murder, sexual immorality, violence, hopelessness and all forms of wickedness, both man-made and natural disasters were signs Jesus identified for us to watch for (Mathew 24).

All these point to the beginning of the end. The world we live in was not built to last forever. There is a Kingdom of God that lasts for eternity. Jesus said, *"In My Father's house are many mansions; if it were not so, I would have told you. I go to prepare a place for you (John 14:2).*

The flight to the Kingdom of God is the main focus of this book. And you are invited to join in. My dear reader, you may belong to the other category of readers this book is written for. You may not have been washed of the blood of Jesus that qualifies all passengers for the final flight.

I believe the grace of God is sufficient for you and that's why you are reading this book. Everyone who believes in Jesus and has received Him into their heart as

Lord and savior has the ticket to this glorious flight. You too can get yours today.

My prayer for you is that even before you finish reading this book, you will take a few minutes before God.

Acknowledge you are a sinner because of your actions and because the entire human race is under condemnation as a result of sin committed by our Adamic root as the bible says.

Jesus paid the ransom for all our sins with His blood and death on Calvary Cross. Yes, Jesus shed His blood and died for you so you can live eternally with God. He is the flight ticket for the final flight. He is the passport to the heavenly destination – the kingdom of God.

You ask God for the forgiveness of sin. You believe in the sacrifice of love He made when He sent Jesus to come to the world and die on the cross for you. You repent from sin and you ask Jesus to come into your life as you make Him your personal Lord and savior.

You will become a child of God. You will become born again. You will be granted entry for the final flight when Jesus returns for those who believe in Him. It is that simple. Do it now! Say this prayer:

"Father in heaven, You are the creator of everything in existence. You made me in your own image. By my actions, I confess to you I have sinned. By the reason of my being part of the human race, I confess that I am a sinner.

For your word says that all people have sinned and have come short of your glory. I believe that with His blood that He shed on Calvary Cross when He died, Jesus Christ paid the ransom for my redemption from sin into eternal relationship with you, Father God.

I ask for your forgiveness now. I repent from my sins. Jesus, come into my heart, as I make

you my personal Lord and Savior. I thank you Father God for forgiving me.

Finally, it is my prayer and hope that by reading all the revelations given to me by the Lord Jesus and my personal testimonies regarding this soon-to-happen event, you will in turn be a crusader for the subject as you share in church on the pulpit and the pew, in your office, in the news and market places as Jesus is just about to appear in the sky to harvest His faithful believers away from the world.

It is also my prayer and hope that you will receive direct revelations on the subject from Jesus. It is for the reasons of the revelations given and the Lord's instructions on them regarding His imminent return that I have created a dedicated website for everything on the subject of The Final Flight.

At RUWEMI Ministries, we are embarking on The Final Flight video production that focuses attention on the subject to invite the world to receive Jesus and to remind His believers to be ready for His coming. Join the cause at www.thefinalflight.org.

CHAPTER 1- I WAS TAKEN UP

It was on Friday November 25, 2016 at about 8:30pm. Whyte Avenue is a notorious party strip in Edmonton. Like most Friday nights, I would go to the Whyte to preach the gospel to the lost. But for a couple of weeks, I observed a necessary detour at the church I attend on my Friday night routine.

A German and a French evangelist had recently started a church service on Friday nights. I would go partly to receive their blessings before heading for the street and partly to keep them encouraged as you may know, church attendance is usually low on weekdays, not alone on a Friday night.

That faithful night, I was already too late to make the service as I have had to carry out a diaper duty and tuck my little ones to bed. But I still wanted to make some appearance at the service before leaving for the streets just to encourage these faithful servants of God.

As I got to the door of the sanctuary, I spotted the usual faces in attendance seated in front of the sanctuary including the leading evangelists, wife and husband. "Joshua, come on in here, we are done praying. We are just meditating and waiting to see if the Lord will have something to say to us. Grab a chair" The evangelist beckoned me in and got me a chair.

We were 7 in total. I sat down, closed my eyes, prayed and joined the group in the quiet listening session. Within minutes, something extra-ordinary happened to me. I saw myself being taken up from the group. I opened my eyes intermittently to see if this was real, I could still see the remaining people seated in the group.

But I kept traveling far up from realm to realm away from the earth. I was having an out-of-body experience. And at this point I knew I was being transported. I had heard the story of a pastor that once was transported. The travel continued until suddenly I found myself on top of what looks like a mighty rock.

Beside the rock is another massive rock, far higher than the one I was standing on. I looked down below the rock that I stood on and I saw a sea of river like crystal clear glass. In the creation account from the book of genesis in the bible, God made the firmament (heaven), and divided the waters which were under the firmament from the waters which were above the firmament (Genesis 1:6-8).

So indeed, there are rivers above the atmospheric existence of the earth and they are in no way related to precipitation that brings rain or snow. Somehow, I have crossed that river to get on top of the rock. How I did this, I have no idea.

Suddenly and spontaneously, I burst into singing with tears rolling down my eyes. I looked and for some reason I

My experience on top of the big rock away from the earthly realm continued.

was still able to see the people seated with me on the earth in the church service. When I burst into singing, they joined me in singing because it was a familiar song to them.

The brethren in this service later confirmed that they joined me in singing and that they knew something was happening to me. They just did not know what exactly it was.

Till today, none of us remember the exact song we sang that night. As soon as we finished singing the song and we stopped, my experience on top of the big rock away from the earthly realm continued.

I looked up to the higher, adjacent rock to the one I was standing. I heard from on top of it classical songs of worship to God by people. The voices sounded human and angelic as though the angels joined the people to worship. It was the most beautiful thing I have heard.

At this point, it occurred to me that somebody would have to come from among those singing on the other rock to come get me to join them. But the lead evangelist at the evening service on the earth felt the need to close the service as it was getting late.

As he grabbed the microphone announcing the service was over, I disengaged from this whole experience. But I got to the border of paradise. I will explain to you later in this book.

However, I knew it would happen again as the story did not finish. We quietly greeted each other. And I thought perhaps others experienced the same thing. My unplanned adventure was abruptly interrupted. For some reason, I was convinced it would happen again, perhaps because I knew that the story had not ended.

And it did happen again. This time, it was a dream vision on February 14, 2017. In the vision, I was walking on the pedestrian lane. Suddenly, a fast-moving oncoming lorry truck seemed to be deliberately leaving the road. It climbed the curb on the pedestrian lane to hit me. It was too late for me to make a retreat and I thought I was going to die.

Just before the impact, somebody suddenly grabbed me away from the scene of what could have been a fatal accident and off we traveled up again. I was carried like a baby and into the sky away from the earth. We kept journeying up and at some point, we hit an ocean and kept journeying up the ocean.

I was made to see the seabed with seashells as though to convince me I was in a river. All through it, I never felt cold as the body of the one holding me was warm. Then as it was with my experience of November 25, 2016 when I burst into a spontaneous worship song, this time it was worship of words to the one holding me: "My Lord and savior Jesus, I love you. Let me see your face".

We kept going up the ocean as though we would hit the dry land or an open air when I woke up from the vision. I must tell you that prior to these two revelations, I had seen the Lord Jesus in dreams and revelations. In some of them, He was demonstrating to me that His return to the world is just about to happen.

He would appear to me in the sky and show me the nail marks on His palms as evidence it is Jesus. I believe that Jesus was using this to demonstrate to me and everyone, that one of bible's most important doctrinal prophecies, the coming of Jesus and the Final Flight of His believers is just about to happen, sooner than anyone could ever imagine.

I will give further explanation of the open vision that was repeated in a dream vision which I described above, in later chapters. Let me give you two more messages from Jesus that further demonstrates this point on the urgency of His return.

Jesus gave me a dream-vision, showing me the entry of the antichrist into the world in just the same way John the Beloved describes it in chapter 13 of the Book of Revelation.

On December 6, 2016, 11 days after I was taken up in the open vision described above, Jesus gave me a dream-vision, showing me the entry of the antichrist into the world in just the same way John the Beloved describes it in chapter 13 of the Book of Revelation.

The antichrist is the man of lawlessness and he will rule the world in a period described as the Great Tribulation, starting immediately after Jesus takes away His believers from this world in the final flight. More on the antichrist later in this book.

2017 jubilee appears to be the end of the waiting period for Jesus' return

The other message from Jesus that reinforces the closeness of His return came on January 22, 2017. Jesus told me that 2017 is jubilee year. As I explain later in this book, a jubilee year marks the end, the completion or the fullness of one time-period and the beginning of a new one.

In the context of the Lord's revelation to me, 2017 jubilee appears to be the end of the waiting period for Jesus' return and any moment from now, Jesus may return for the final flight. The clock is ticking. I pray that you and I will not miss the flight with Jesus.

CHAPTER 2 – THE FINAL FLIGHT - BIBLE

I was not the only one that was taken up in the way described above. I know of another servant of God that testified he too was transported. A great woman of God, Mary Baxter, recounts in her books, how Jesus took her in repeated visits to Hell for 30 days and to heaven for 10 days. I will touch on Baxter's experience later.

> *"For the Lord Himself will descend from heaven with a shout, with the voice of an archangel, and with the trumpet of God. And the dead in Christ will rise first.* [17]*
>
> *Then we who are alive and remain shall be caught up together with them in the clouds to meet the Lord in the air. And thus we shall always be with the Lord."(1 Thessalonians 4:16-18)*

Let's look at a few prior occurrences of the final flight of the saints of God that Paul describes in 1 Thessalonians 4 above. Several righteous people in the bible had experienced the same. The bible records that Enoch was a righteous man. Instead of experiencing death like others when his time on the earth was over, he was taken up by God (Genesis 5).

Elijah the prophet was a righteous man. When his earthly journey ended, the bible records he was taken up in a whirlwind to heaven (2Kings 2).

Before Elijah's departure, God had revealed to about 50 of his fellow prophets that he would be taken up. His servant Elisha watched Elijah suddenly taken up by a chariot of fire with horses of fire in a whirlwind to heaven.

About 4o days after His resurrection, Jesus Christ Himself ascended into heaven with His followers watching Him being gradually swallowed up through the skies of Bethany (Luke 24, Acts 1:9-12).

All these occurrences including those recorded in the bible and those in books by believers in this church age, are God's foreshadow of how all the saints of God will journey from the earth to the Kingdom of God.

Invitation extended to every human being

There is presently a great expectation for this soon-to-happen epochal event in the realm of the spirit. Jesus desires that His believers on the earth will have the same expectation.

The invitation to this powerful, glorious and exciting journey is extended to every human being. The flight ticket is the blood Jesus shed on Calvary Cross for the sin of the world.

Only those who have the ticket will qualify for the journey. Only those who have repented from sin, have received forgiveness of sin through the washing of the blood of Jesus, have been born again, will be able to go with Jesus in the final flight. Only those who have Jesus in them as their Lord and Savior will be able to fly with Him.

There is an African saying, "it is what the bird has eaten that it would use to fly". Yes, it is the Jesus in you that will enable your involvement in this glorious flight at the end. If you do not have Jesus, I urge you to receive Him as your Lord now. If you know people who do not have Jesus, I urge you to invite them to receive Jesus now.

If you are a believer of Jesus, and you have not been actively waiting for His return by vertically looking up for the fulfillment of His promise and horizontally looking at your surroundings to tell others about Him, I urge you to begin to, or intensify your effort on this.

> *"It is what the bird has eaten that it would use to fly". You need Jesus in you to fly*

Look at how the disciple Luke describes what happened when Jesus ascended into heaven in broad view of his disciples:

> *"Now when He had spoken these things, while they watched, He was taken up, and a cloud received Him out of their sight.*
>
> *And while they looked steadfastly toward heaven as He went up, behold, two men stood by them in white apparel who also said,*
>
> *"Men of Galilee, why do you stand gazing up into heaven? This same Jesus, who was taken up from you into heaven, will so come in like manner as you saw Him go into heaven." (Acts 1:9-11)*

The two men that appeared to the disciples were angels. In saying Jesus will come in the same manner as He ascends to heaven, they echoed the message of Jesus' appearance in the sky that Paul would later reveal in greater detail in his writing to the Corinthian and Thessalonian churches (1 Corinthians 15, I Thessalonians 4, 5).

The message of the return of Jesus and the final flight of His believers is referenced in several books of the Old Testament. For example, Daniel mentioned this in his prophecy of the end time (Daniel 12).

It is of course referenced in all 4 gospels of the New Testament. Almost all the epistle writers, including Peter, James, John, Paul and Luke referenced this important soon-to-happen event.

*2017 was a significant year that marked the
end of a spiritual era and the start of another*

CHAPTER 3 - 2017 – THE YEAR OF JUBILEE

Something else the Holy Spirit is using to show you and I that Jesus will soon appear in the sky for His believers is the prophetic word He gave for 2017. I lay down. It was on Sunday, January 22, 2017, at exactly 12:00pm. The Holy Spirit said to me "Joshua, 2017 is Jubilee Year".

Unpacking this prophetic declaration in the context of Leviticus 25, a jubilee year is a year of repentance, redemption, restoration, restitution, reconciliation and readiness for a new beginning, and in the context of this book, the final flight of the saints of Jesus.

After giving this prophetic word, the Holy Spirit specifically directed me to pray for the salvation of souls. Later that week, I went with my family to visit with friends in the city of Calgary. When I narrated what I received about the year to my friends, I witnessed a wife say to her husband "did I not tell you?" She had received the same word.

This prophecy was confirmed severally by other servants of God. The year 2017 is the end of an era and the beginning of another in the realm of the spirit according to God's calendar.

Additionally, it came to public knowledge that 2017 was the fulfillment of the prophecy given by a Jewish Rabbi, Judah Ben Samuel in 1217. The understanding is that Ben Samuel had prophesied that from his time, there will be certain numbers of jubilees before the Messiah returns and 2017, being a jubilee year, is the completion of the predicted number.

2017 is a jubilee year also because in it the nation of Israel, created in 1947, turned 70 years. Anyone who is familiar with God's pattern of doing things would understand that Israel is God's calendar on earth.

For example, Jesus the Messiah paid the ultimate price for sin and our redemption with His life only short of a day before the Jewish Passover commemoration.

In date-calling outbursts – good chance to dive in, present the true gospel

Unfortunately, we live in a world in which properly translating and interpreting the prophetic has become an increasing challenge. And the enemy plunges into this challenge for his own interest.

Some are in the habit of using these specific prophecies to put a date on Jesus' return. This is wrong. It furthers the devil's interest.

September 23, 2017 was pegged as a doomsday by a numerologist. This falsehood went viral globally, although far less than the hype garnered by the Y2K doomsday, end of the world. I immediately recognised this as a work of darkness even before I got to know it was from an astronomer.

Jesus has affirmed that no one, not even the Son, knows the day or the hour when the Son will come, except the Father God in heaven.

The devil's calculation is that if he pegged a date on the fulfillment of the end time prophecies knowing that God would not sanction the date, his deception would deepen the depth of deception that the world is not ending anyway, that Jesus' return is not imminent as His followers claim.

And so people are generally dismissive of any divine revelations suggesting the imminent return of Jesus or the beginning of the end of the world.

What is more concerning is believers' dismissal of divine revelations for the end time simply because of date-calling outbursts that indeed contradict the bible.

The date-calling outbursts are engineered by the devil or by careless believers who misinterpret the prophetic and are taken advantage of by the devil.

But this is not an excuse to ignore the signs as Jesus instructed or the revelations that He gives regarding His return. The date-calling outbursts should be seen by you and I as opportunity to dive in and present the truth to the world.

Yes, no one should know the day or the hour when Jesus returns for the final flight of His believers, marking the beginning of the end of the world.

That Jesus is coming very soon, given the signs He said we should watch for, should be a message aggressively shared during these outbursts.

And these outbursts are not entirely a new phenomenon in this church age. They existed in the generation of the early apostles in the New Testament of the bible.

Paul had to address this controversy in his writing to the Thessalonian church (1 Thessalonians 5). Believers in this generation should follow the example set by Paul during these outbursts.

We should be out to confirm the true message. That very soon, Jesus will take His believers away from the world as promised, marking the beginning of the end of time.

September 23 went viral globally nonetheless. It was the same time at RUWEMI Ministries, we were planning to shoot a video to spotlight the imminent return of Jesus and the Final Flight based on the revelations I describe in this book. Our event was planned for September 29 and 30, dates given in a vision.

I was convinced it was God's timing for the event more because of the word I had received from the Lord in prior months for everything I set out to do in 2017. The event date was set before September 23 became a public knowledge, to the best of my understanding at that time.

I saw September 23 as an opposition from the devil against any event that attempted to direct focus on the coming of Jesus and the end times.

And I could see the opposition against our September 29 and 30 events in the planning and execution. But I made sure to obey God's instruction notwithstanding the very few people that turned up for it. And thanks to God, we will shoot the video this year.

I am not a numerologist. But let me play on numbers a little bit and share with you one divine perspective to numbers. 2017 is two thousand and seventeen years.

A day is like a thousand years in the eyes of God, the bible says (Psalm 90:4, 2 Peter 3:8). This will translate to mean that 2017 is 2 days and some, perhaps, 17 minutes, in God's eternity calendar and how He measures time. This at least shows God operates with numbers.

Also, the number 7 in the realm of the spirit signifies completion, fullness, finality. There are 7 spirits of God. I recall some time ago when I went through a valley experience.

As believers, we sometimes go through experiences that are not God's ultimate desire for us, but He allows us to go through them in order to strengthen our relationship with Him. In such difficult valley experiences, God has our attention the most.

The Lord taught me quite a lot of things over the course of almost two years in this valley state. He made promises to me that it would soon be over. One and a half years has elapsed. Yet I had not seen the light at the end of the tunnel. The bible says hope that delays makes the heart go sick. But a desire fulfilled is like a tree of life.

My heart began to grow faint even though I still trusted in the Lord's promises. I was taking a walk one afternoon along the river valley of my neighborhood. Jesus interrupted my worry with the following words:

> *"Joshua, you remember the scripture that I gave you about a year ago, 'Mark the upright man and observe the blameless, the end of that man shall be peace', Psalm 37:37".*

> *I said yes Lord. "That scripture", He continued, "is deliberately 37: 37 to show that the decision concerning the righteous man was not without witnesses.*

> *It was an agreement and a conclusion between God the Father, God the Son and God the Holy Spirit. That explains the number 3.*

> *Number 7 signifies completion or conclusion in the realm of the spirit. It is firmly decided in the mind of God and it is final that the end of the righteous man shall be peace".*

That is the Holy Spirit revealing that numbers are symbolic to the trinity and in the realm of the spirit.

As I described earlier on, just before 2017, in November 2016, I was taken up in a vision to a place I now know is the border of paradise.

A few days later in December 2016, Jesus gave me a vision in which the Antichrist was revealed to the world. In January 2017, I was told by the Holy Spirit that 2017 is Jubilee year. In February 2017, Jesus repeated the open vision on a journey with Him to paradise in a dream-vision.

Jesus used this to demonstrate to me that first, paradise is real and that the final flight of His believers would be the same way I traveled with Him, but by then, it would be with our glorified body.

A couple of months later, He appeared to me in a vision promising to take me to the kingdom of God but charged me not to slow down in preaching the gospel.

Putting all of these together, you would understand why all of my veins, arteries, spirit, soul and body felt that His return is very imminent as it would happen any moment from now.

I never pegged a date on it. Jesus did not. If He did, it would not be Jesus. Jesus would always give the spoken word (rhema) in line with the written word of the bible (logo). But 2017 is undoubtedly a significant year that marked the end of a spiritual era and the beginning of another.

A vertical focus on the promise of Jesus' return propels a horizontal focus on His message to us

So, I believe the Final Flight will happen anytime from now. Believing that Jesus may come in the next blink of an eye is the right disposition towards this important subject in the bible notwithstanding the visions and revelations. The bible says:

> *"Behold, I tell you a mystery: We shall not all sleep, but we shall all be changed— in a moment, in the twinkling of an eye, at the last trumpet.*

For the trumpet will sound, and the dead will be raised incorruptible, and we shall be changed" (1Corinthians 50-52).

The early believers in the New Testament of the bible had the same disposition. They were vertically focused, looking up to the promise of the return of Jesus for His kingdom.

This propelled them to be horizontally focused on the preaching of His kingdom in the Great Commission. God is calling our attention to a vertical focus on the return of His Son Jesus. This should be a driving denominator for our horizontal commitment to reach the lost.

> During the reign of the antichrist, grace for
> repentance will be like a drop in the ocean.

CHAPTER 4 – I SAW THE ANTICHRIST

On that fateful day of the 6th of December 2016, I saw in the dream-vision Jesus gave me, two fishermen had just caught a big fish and they were trying to sell it by the river banks. A man approached to buy the fish and a transaction was set in motion.

As the transaction progresses, the fish began to roar like a lion and it changed its head to a bear, to a lion, to a fish again and kept changing its head to different kinds of wild animals.

I warned the folks standing by including the purchaser that the fish looked strange and should not be eaten. As the transaction progresses to a close, the roar from the fish grew louder and louder. As soon as the transaction was complete and $20 was paid for it, the fish stood up and became a giant man.

The giant beastly man began walking into the mainland and swearing, saying all sorts of blasphemies, cursing God to the point of being so offensive to people around. Then two of the men standing by who were offended by his blasphemies ran towards him to prevent him from going to the mainland.

When they got to him, the giant beat them up with a super-human strength only with one hand. He threw the two men to the wall. They hit the wall, fell down and began coughing. As though they realized it was a serious situation, someone said to others to call 911.

In response, the beastly giant boasted that he would lock the police up. Then at this point. I woke up from the dream with a serious migraine, consistent with what happens when God is giving me a serious message.

As soon as I woke up, the first thought the Holy Spirit gave me came out of my mouth in form of a question. I began asking myself, "is that the antichrist? What a dream?" A few seconds later, the Holy Spirit reminded me of a scripture I had read long before, that talks about an animal coming out of the river.

I could not remember the exact scripture and so I googled. It was revelations 13. Exactly what I saw in my dream was the beast (the antichrist) coming out of the river in this passage of the scriptures.

Prior to this terrifying dream-vision, the subject of the antichrist was never in my thoughts, prayers or routine actions for at least months, if not years. So, the dream vision was not a product of my thoughts or imagination.

It was a revelation from Jesus. After Jesus takes the rest of His believers from the world, the antichrist, the man of lawlessness, will take over and rule the world globally in a one-world government, for seven years.

He will first pretend to be a man of peace, the expected Messiah by the Jewish people, and deceiving many people. He will later position himself as God. Then he will begin to inflict horror on those who live on the earth in what is known as the Great Tribulation.

Grace for repentance to salvation is now like an ocean. During the reign of the antichrist, grace for repentance will be like a drop in the ocean. Buying and selling will not be possible unless you have allowed on your forehead or on your arm the mark of the beast. The intensity of the forceful and violent horror of the antichrist would be too much for any human strength to bear. The faithful preachers on earth would have all left with Jesus.

It would be the angels' turn to proclaim the eternal gospel to those on the earth, as written in the book of revelation (Revelations 14: 6).

But the angels' gospel will come with warning to people not to receive the mark of the beast. There will be no redemption from eternal doom for anyone who accepts the mark of the beast. Satan will have his legal right permanently on them.

Yes, a few will bear it and together with the elect remnant of Israel, they will be taken away with Jesus during His second coming to the world. Now is the time of salvation. The next minute might be too late.

> *"I am the resurrection and the life. He who*
> *believes in Me, though he may die, he shall live"*

CHAPTER 5 – JESUS AND THE DEAD RISE

Paul, Peter, Luke, John, and all the New Testament writers of the bible focused on the risen Christ as the hope of eternal life for everyone who believes in Him. Empowered by the Holy Spirit, testimony that Jesus is risen from the dead birthed the early New Testament church. It is the fact of Jesus' resurrection that guarantees the resurrection of the dead.

In John 11, Jesus repeatedly says "I am the resurrection and the life. He who believes in Me, though he may die, he shall live." As I describe later in this book, the resurrection of the righteous dead will be one of the great events that will mark the appearance of Jesus for the final flight of His believers.

But let's examine both events together here – resurrection of Jesus the Christ and the later resurrection of His righteous people. Thomas Nelson, Publishers of the New King James Version of the bible, write in their introduction to the book of Acts:

> *"The extraordinary growth of the early*
> *church was based directly on the*
> *resurrected Christ[...] The early Christians*
> *were not testifying about a dead Christ, but*

> *a living Christ whom they had seen with their own eyes" (NKJV 1705).*

Without a doubt, even in this church age of the 21st Century, the resurrection of Jesus is generally regarded, and rightly so, as bible's most important doctrine, though it may not be seen in practice.

What is also true is that resurrection of Christ reopened the long-held doctrine on the resurrection of the dead which was a controversy among the Pharisees and Sadducees.

Paul eloquently used this controversy in a divide and rule strategy to escape from his accusers when he perceived they were Pharisees, who believed in the resurrection of the dead, and Sadducees, who did not (Acts 23). The Sadducees contended with the Pharisees principally over the latter's belief in the resurrection of the dead.

My thought on this difference in belief on resurrection is that perhaps the Pharisees paid more attention, more curiosity and more time into learning what they read from the scriptures including the prophets and the law, just like the more noble Berean Jews Paul describes in Acts 17 who were more curious about what they have learned.

Both groups believed that Elijah would someday come back to the earth. From what they read in the prophets, the same Elijah raised the widow's son from the dead. Then you wonder why the Sadducees would still have a trouble believing there would someday be the resurrection of the dead.

Being influenced by a religious spirit as the Sadducees were, might sometimes result in a loss of common reasoning. My prayer for you and myself is that we will be free from every influence of the religious spirit in Jesus name.

The bible is full of the message of the resurrection of Jesus the Messiah and the resurrection of the dead. For example in Psalm 16:10, David referenced Jesus as one not subject to decay after death. David died and his body decayed. Jesus later confirms He was the one David was talking about.

Jesus died on the cross. His body did not see decay in the grave. He came back to life on the third day and He ascended to heaven with a glorified body. As of this moment, Jesus sits at the right hand of God in heaven. That is the unassailable hope of eternal life for everyone who believes in Him.

Before He went to the Cross to pay the ultimate sacrifice for the sin of all of mankind, Jesus is the resurrection that had become a subject of debate and controversy between the Pharisees and Sadducees. Just before He raised His dear friend Lazarus from death to life, He confirms to Martha: "I am the resurrection and the Life" (John 11).

One of the main thrust of this book as you will see more later, is to possibly spark a revolution, an extension of focus beyond the resurrection of Jesus which has been deemed as the most important doctrine. Pay attention to this: the resurrection of Jesus foreshadowed what is to come.

Yes, the resurrection of Jesus was a foreshadow of the resurrection of the dead. Hence, Jesus desires we extend our focus on His resurrection to the resurrection of the righteous dead which will soon happen just before the boarding process for the final flight.

Resurrection of the dead is one of bible's most important subjects and should be regarded as such. The resurrection of Jesus happened because of the resurrection of the dead. I am not talking about a dead son raised to life by Elijah. I am not talking about Lazarus, raised to life by Jesus.

Even when Jesus rose from the dead on the third day, He brought many dead people with Him who came to life.

I am not talking about the raising of a dead son by Elijah or the raising of Lazarus from death to life by Jesus. I'm not talking about Jesus Christ coming to life

> *Resurrection of the dead should then be*
> *Seen as the most important bible subject*

on the 3rd day after His death. Not about Paul raising to life Eutychus who was sleeping while Paul preached and fell from the window top into death. I'm not talking about the missionary evangelist to Africa, Reinhard Bonnke raising the dead to life in Jesus' name.

All these are faith pillars to enable our belief and preparation for something prophetically and profoundly greater and that will soon happen.

According to the Lord's own word to me that the glory of the latter days will surpass the former, you can expect that several more of these events with the dead coming to life, will happen in these end times.

These miraculous events of resurrection were meant to foreshadow what Jesus intends to do at the resurrection of the dead. I'm talking about the final resurrection of all those who have died righteous which will happen at the appearance of Jesus in the sky just before the final flight of all His believers from this world into the heavenly kingdom.

I pray for you and myself that we will make the final flight. Resurrection of the dead should then be considered as the most important bible subject. And it should be the most important doctrine for our benefits also because it is happening at the same time as the final flight of the saints.

In response to it, Jesus says, "I am the resurrection and the life". In response to it, Jesus went to the cross, died and rose on the third day as a proof that He is the resurrection and the life".

In response to it, Jesus raised many from the dead to life. In response to it, He still raises the dead to life till today through His believers. See how Paul in the bible underscores the significance of this event when writing to the Corinthian church:

"Now if Christ is preached that He has been
raised from the dead, how do some among you
say that there is no resurrection of the dead?
But if there is no resurrection of the dead,
then Christ is not risen.

And if Christ is not risen, then our preaching
is empty and your faith is also empty. Yes, and
we are found false witnesses of God, because
we have testified of God that He raised up

Christ, whom He did not raise up - if in fact
the dead do not rise. For if the dead do not rise,
then Christ is not risen. And if Christ is not
risen, your faith is futile;

you are still in your sins! Then also those who
have fallen asleep in Christ have perished.
If in this life only we have hope in Christ, we
are of all men the most pitiable"(1 Corin-
thians 15:12-19)

The early church experienced an unprecedented revival partly because their eyes were vertically focused on the coming of the Lord Jesus, the resurrection of the dead, and the final flight of His saints.

This enabled their eyes to be horizontally focused to carry out the Great Commission to preach the gospel to every nation with signs and wonders following. In our church age, thanks to God, we have witnessed multiple periods of great revival.

However, in Sunday services, bible school, Sunday schools and bible studies, I sense the need that we need a redirection to this vertical and horizontal focus to again experience a greater dimension of revival, not alone the imminent need to prepare ourselves for the Lord's coming as the day draws nearer.

> *This at the very least indicates that Jesus had Moses in mind when He said no one has been to heaven except Him, Jesus*

CHAPTER 6 – ARE THE RIGHTEOUS DEAD IN HEAVEN?

The bible clearly describes what will happen to the righteous dead when Jesus appears to take us away in the final flight. The dead in Christ will rise first to meet the Lord in the air before those who are alive will join this most important voyage. (1 Thessalonians 4:16). But I suppose you, like many others, would wonder: why then do Christians say the dead in Christ have gone to be with Jesus in heaven?

If the dead in Christ are in heaven with Jesus, why then would they still rise from the dead to meet with Jesus in the air for the journey? I have also wondered the same way in the past before the Lord opened my eyes through the scriptures, His instructions and the visions He gave me.

Some people have in error, or in deliberate spread of heresies, resorted to insist that the righteous dead remain in the grave and that their souls do not exist until, and unless there is resurrection.

The same enemies of the Cross of Jesus claim there is no place called hell, hence, as they claim, no consequence for the sinner, if he chooses to reject the kingdom of God through Jesus Christ.

This is a lie from the pit of hell designed to keep sinners in deceit and entrap them into the devil's temporary home in hell when they die. They also claim that healing miracles stopped with the New Testament disciples in the bible, but no longer exist in our generation.

But I am an eye witness to healing miracles and I saw the blind receive their sight, the lame walk and the deaf hear. When I was a teenager, I also miraculously received instant healing on my left foot from an injury sustained while playing soccer. I got healed when the preacher prayed in Jesus name.

These people are spreading lies when they are dismissive of miraculous healing. They are painstaking in their commitment to the spread of a tainted gospel of the kingdom. I do not hesitate to give them audience to engage them in the hope that by speaking, some may be rescued from the coming Lake of Fire for deceiving many into it.

Some of them are victims of deceit themselves and may be sincerely wrong. So, they need our prayers. Others are in the know of these destructive heresies and are serving their master Lucifer.

You may have run into them already. They knock on doors from house to house. They put on tie and are smartly dressed. They are generally accepted by the world without opposition to their gospel because Satan, the prince of this world benefits from their actions.

The next time you see them, present the truth to them in love and try to bring them to the light of Jesus. They are trained argumentators. You may as well put on your running shoes to run as fast as you can before they steal eternity with God from you.

Again, I couldn't resist a holy digression tempered with righteous offense. After all, it is our Father's kingdom. If His business is being run down by others, it should concern us. Let's go back to determine whether the righteous dead are in heaven.

I pray that the Holy Spirit will open the eyes of your heart to receive answers to this important question as He did for me and would have me share with you. First, look at Jesus' response to the complement He received from Nicodemus, a pharisaic Jewish ruler:

> *"...Most assuredly, I say to you, unless one is born again, he cannot see the kingdom of God." (John 3:3).*

Jesus proceeds to explain what this means:

> *"Most assuredly, I say to you, unless one is born of water and the Spirit, he cannot enter the kingdom of God (John 3:5).*

This means that there is a kingdom of God and the only way anyone can enter it is to be born again. And to be born again is to be born of water and of the Spirit. To be born of water and of the Spirit is to first confess our sins and believe in the sacrifice Jesus made for our redemption from them on Calvary Cross with His blood and death.

It is then the spirit of Jesus, the Holy Spirit gives us a new spirit as we are first spirit beings who live in a body and have a soul. When we have a new spirit, we are born again. We have been born of water and of the Spirit. Then we qualify to enter the Kingdom of God. Praise God!

But is this Kingdom of God that Jesus refers to different from heaven? Let's pay attention to this note in the same passage of the scripture. Watch what Jesus later said to Nicodemus:

> *"If I have told you earthly things and you do not believe, how will you believe if I tell you heavenly things?*

38

> *No one has ascended to heaven but He who*
> *came down from heaven, that is, the Son of*
> *Man who is in heaven" (John 3:12-13).*

The Kingdom of God referred to here is what I call the 4th heaven in this book. And from Jesus' statement, it can't be any clearer that no one has ascended to this heaven, except Him, Jesus. Not even the prophets of old have ascended to heaven except Jesus the Son of God who came down from heaven.

Another holy digression: Jesus indicates in this scripture that while on earth, He was fully man and fully God.

As at the time Jesus made this statement, no one, none of the righteous dead has ascended to this heaven. Though not part of the focus of this book, for those who are in doubt of the trinity and the belief that Jesus was fully human and fully divine when He walked the surface of the earth, I urge you to use the side note in this scripture to explain to them: *"No one has ascended to heaven but He who came down from heaven, that is, the Son of Man who is in heaven"*.

Jesus the Son of Man standing right there with Nicodemus on the earth, demonstrated His omniscience (all-knowing God), and omnipresence (all-present God). Jesus the Son of man came down from heaven (past). Jesus the Son of Man standing with Nicodemus (present). Jesus the Son of Man *who is in heaven* right now, even though He is standing with Nicodemus (present). I just couldn't resist the temptation for that holy digression.

Let's go back on track to our focus on the righteous dead. Was Jesus exaggerating when He said that no one has been to heaven? No. He is a truth-teller. Jesus never for once lied. He is a super duper gut-wrenching truth-teller.

For example, He was asked about the time when He will return for the final flight. Jesus said He didn't know the exact day except the Father in heaven. He had the chance to defend His omniscience to His disciples by giving a date. He did not, because the Father in heaven had not revealed the date to Him. That was even when His reputation as the all-knowing God was as stake.

Now, notice in the same passage what He said further in the next verse: *"And as Moses lifted up the serpent in the wilderness, even so must the Son of Man be lifted up, that whoever believes in Him should not perish but have eternal life" (John 3:15).*

This at the very least indicates that Jesus had Moses in mind when He said no one has been to heaven except Jesus Himself. So, Jesus did not forget Moses when he said no one has been to heaven. He knew that Moses was not in heaven or the Kingdom of God. Neither is Abraham, Isaac and Jacob and all the Old Testament prophets and righteous saints, in the kingdom of God.

See, for example, the apostle Peter affirming that the righteous king David is not in heaven after testifying that Jesus went to Hades from where He was exalted to the right hand of God in heaven:

> *"For David did not ascend into the heavens, but he says himself: The Lord said to my Lord, sit at My right hand, till I make Your enemies Your footstool."* (Acts 2:34-35).

So, if David did not ascend into the heavens, and only Jesus did, is David still in the grave since the time He died? The answer is no!

So where are the righteous dead of the Old Testament, the dead in Christ in the early church of the New Testament and the departed believers of Jesus in the 21st Century church? Where are the righteous dead of the Old Testament if, as Jesus indicates, even Moses has not entered heaven?

And if the New Testament dead believers are already in the heavenly kingdom, or in heaven, why would the dead in Christ still have to rise to life again at the appearance of Jesus for the final flight, as Paul describes in 1 Thessalonians 4:16?

No one has been to the heavenly kingdom of God except Jesus the one who came from there. Watch what Jesus says about entering the Kingdom of God through Him (the narrow gate):

> *"There will be weeping and gnashing of teeth, when you see Abraham and Isaac and Jacob and all the prophets in the kingdom of God, and yourselves thrust out.*
>
> *They will come from the east and the west, from the north and the south, and sit down in the kingdom of God. And indeed there are last who will be first, and there are first who will be last." (Luke 13:28-30).*

Jesus just describes what will happen when believers arrive at the marriage supper of the Lamb in the Kingdom. The wicked and the sinful dead will also want to get in but they do not have Jesus, the passport to the heavenly country.

But notice what Jesus says about Abraham, Isaac and Jacob, and by extension, all the righteous dead of the Old Testament.

They will have arrived from a journey from the East, North and South to the Kingdom of God. This means that they are not in the Kingdom of God yet. They will arrive from the final flight of all the saints of God into the heavenly Kingdom – the 4th heaven.

Here, all the saints will be welcomed by a great feast, a banquet prepared by Jesus, also known as the marriage supper of the Lamb.

So where then are the righteous dead? Notice again what Jesus says:

> *"I am the good shepherd; and I know My sheep and am known by My own. As the Father knows Me, even so I know the Father; and I lay down My life for the sheep.*
>
> *And other sheep I have which are not of this fold; them also I must bring, and they will hear My voice; and there will be one flock and one shepherd" (John 10:16).*

Jesus is certainly not referring to the would-be believers when He says other sheep I have which are not of this fold otherwise he won't say He already has them as His sheep. He was referring to the sheep of Israel, and the righteous dead in the Old Testament.

They are not of the same fold in the New Testament dispensation. But they too belong to Jesus. And since Jesus is the only way, truth and the life to the kingdom of God, they will need Jesus to bring them with us to become one flock.

> *Jesus restored us into a relationship with*
> *God better than the one that existed then*

CHAPTER 7 – WHERE THEN ARE THE RIGHTEOUS DEAD NOW?

While on the Cross of Calvary where He paid the death penalty for Sin, two notorious thieves were also being crucified with Jesus. One of them acknowledged himself as a sinner deserving of death but acknowledged Jesus as the savior and Lord.

The thief made a simple request: *"Lord, remember me when you get to your kingdom"*. He received an emphatic answer: *"And Jesus said to him, "Assuredly, I say to you, today you will be with Me in Paradise." (Luke 23:42-43).*

The word "paradise" was also referenced in two other instances in the bible. Paul writing to the Corinthian church describes his knowledge of a man who was caught up into the third heaven (2 Corinthians 12:2). John the Beloved explicitly quotes Jesus saying the word again in His message to the seven churches in Asia:

> *"He who has an ear, let him hear what the Spirit says to the churches. To him who overcomes, I will give to eat from the tree of life, which is in the midst of the Paradise of God."*

With the tree of life in this paradise that Jesus is promising to the saints of the seven churches in Asia, whom He knew would someday die, you can conveniently say that my position in this book that paradise is the Garden of Eden, is supported.

Jesus repeatedly said to the seven churches: "to him who overcomes, I will give to eat from the tree of life, which is in the midst of the paradise of God". After the fall in the Garden of Eden as written in Genesis, Adam and Eve were driven out and prevented from eating from the tree of life. And an angel, a cherubim, was posted to guard the Garden (Genesis 3:24).

So, when Jesus says in this scripture He would give the saints of the seven churches in Asia to eat from the tree of life in the paradise of God, He was indeed referring to the tree of life in the Garden of Eden.

So, Eden is paradise. And all the saints that have departed from the earth have been restored to the original relationship with God in the Garden of Eden (paradise).

But God's redemptive plan for us is not limited to the original relationship we had with Him in the earthly life and glory. The plan is to place us above and beyond to be seated in the heavenly realms in Christ Jesus.

It is always said and believed that Jesus restored us back to a relationship that existed between God and mankind before the fall into sin. Not exactly!

Watch this, Jesus restored us into a relationship with God better than the one that existed before the fall of Adam. Before the fall, God only visited with Adam and Eve in the cool of the beautiful Garden of Eden, which I call God's summer village.

And Jesus now does exactly that as He visits with the saints in paradise from the heavenly kingdom – the 4th heaven. A good indication that Jesus visits this summer village is His revelation of the episode of the rich man

Lazarus in Abraham's bosom, which I have described in this book as another name Jesus uses to describe paradise.

With Jesus as the mediator, God did not just restore us back to the Garden of Eden or paradise, or Abraham's bosom, which is now inhabited by righteous saints that have left the earth. Jesus has promoted our relationship.

And all the saints will be transported either from the earth or from this Garden of Eden, to the heavenly kingdom when Jesus comes for the final flight. The righteous dead who are currently in paradise, their temporary residents, will join with believers who are alive on the earth when Jesus comes, to finally relocate to the Kingdom of God – the 4th heaven. Yes, Jesus restored us into a closer relationship with God than the one before the fall. Praise be to God!

From this point forward, we will permanently dwell with God even when He creates a new heaven and a new earth as John the beloved records in Revelation 21.

The Greek transliteration of the word "paradise" is *"paradeisos"*, which means a park, a garden, a pleasure ground, a well-watered grove, a place of happiness. With the oriental origin of the word are several root words which include an "Eden".

Others simply call it heaven. My open vision experience described in Chapter 1 and the scriptures support all of these understandings of the word paradise, the people in it and where it is located.

Let's examine the scriptures for all of the viewpoints on the word. The episode of Jesus on Calvary Cross with the thief already proves that there is a place called paradise.

It also proves that Jesus went to paradise as soon as He died same day. Remember, one of the two notorious thieves on the Cross with Jesus said to Him *"[...] Lord, remember me when you get to your kingdom." (Luke 23:42)*. Pay attention to the thief's request – *"your kingdom"*.

Now look at Jesus responding to Him: "Assuredly, *I say to you, today you will be with Me in paradise" (Luke 23:43)*. The thief asked to be with Jesus in His "kingdom". Jesus instead promised to take him to "paradise".

Two things you will see here – Jesus went to paradise or Abraham's bosom when He died, as you will see later in this book. Jesus also made a distinction between the kingdom of God and paradise.

And if paradise is adjacent to Hades as claimed and as I will use the scripture to illustrate, then Jesus went to Hades as well on His way to paradise. Jesus went to Hades, where Satan and his demons, the wicked and the sinful dead temporarily reside as I later describe. He went to Hades to complete the payment for our redemption so we do not have to go there.

The wages for our sin is death. We deserved to perish in Hades, a place of great torment being the temporary abode of Satan. Jesus went on our behalf. When He got to Hades, He conquered it and all living in it including Satan. Evidence of His conquest was felt on the earth.

The bible records that at the time Jesus gave up His spirit on Calvary cross, at the time of His death, some very shaking and scary occurrences happened. Look at Mathew's eye witness account of this:

> *"And Jesus cried out again with a loud voice and yielded up His spirit. Then, behold, the veil of the temple was torn in two from top to bottom; and the earth quaked, and the rocks were split, and the graves were opened;*
>
> *and many bodies of the saints who had fallen asleep were raised; and coming out of the graves after His resurrection, they*

> *went into the holy city and appeared to many.*
>
> *So when the centurion and those with him, who were guarding Jesus, saw the earthquake and the things that had happened, they feared greatly, saying, "Truly this was the Son of God!" (Mathew 27:50-54).*

Luke also gives a similar account:

> *"Now it was about the sixth hour, and there was darkness over all the earth until the ninth hour. Then the sun was darkened, and the veil of the temple was torn in two.*
>
> *And when Jesus had cried out with a loud voice, He said, "Father, 'into Your hands I commit My spirit."*
>
> *Having said this, He breathed His last. So when the centurion saw what had happened, he glorified God, saying, "Certainly this was a righteous Man!"*
>
> *And the whole crowd who came together to that sight, seeing what had been done, beat their breasts and returned.*
>
> *But all His acquaintances, and the women who followed Him from Galilee, stood at a distance, watching these things (Luke 23:44-48).*

Both Luke and Mathew indicate a 3-hours of total darkness on the earth while Jesus hung on the Cross, in what should have been a broad day light. Darkness was on the earth because Hades had been invaded by the King of Kings, the Commander of the Lord's Army that Joshua sees (Joshua 5).

The devil, the Prince of the Kingdom of the air as Paul describes him (Ephesians 2), is under siege. Evidence of a cosmic battle is darkness that covered the whole earth. Evidence of Jesus' victory in the cosmic battle is seen with the veil of the temple that was torn in two, the earth that quaked, the rocks that split and Jesus' loud shout with His voice.

Hence Jesus commits His spirit to the Father's hands before exiting the earth (before He dies). He went straight to Hades on our behalf because He already conquered it. And keeping with His promise to the thief on the Cross, He went from Hades to paradise taking the repentant thief along.

Now Mathew provides evidence that Jesus went to paradise on the third day: "and the graves were opened; and many bodies of the saints who had fallen asleep were raised; and coming out of the graves after His resurrection, they went into the holy city [earthly Jerusalem] and appeared to many".

Jesus went to paradise to bring these saints to earth for some unfinished business. Because He is the resurrection and the life, He instructed them in paradise to return to their bodies in the graves and gave their bodies life again notwithstanding the decay.

The saints risen from the dead with Jesus were the prophet Ezekiel's dry bones that came to life on the instruction of Jesus. They were Jesus's entourage when He returned to His own grave on the earth and emerged with a resurrected body on the third day after His death. The Old

Testament prophet Elijah was also returned from paradise to the earth to take care of unfinished business.

Elijah's initial exit from the earth as I mentioned in the 1st chapter was through a chariot of fire. It had to be a chariot of fire as his entire being – body, soul and spirit was transported to paradise. And on the way to, or adjacent to paradise, is Hades which I call the second heaven in this book.

The second heaven, Hades, is the inner extension of Satan's kingdom of the Air, where enemy combatants could have attempted to interrupt Elijah's journey. They did wrestle with and delayed the angel bringing an answer to Daniel's prayer. The angel was coming from the 4th heaven where God dwells (Daniel 10).

In fact the angel conceded to Daniel that he was not strong enough for the prince of Persia (one of Satan's princes), to the point he had to call for reinforcement from the archangel Michael, one of God's mighty generals.

So Elijah had to exit with a chariot of fire to be armed for any onslaught from the kingdom of the air, or its inner dwelling, Hades.

Unlike the saints that resurrected with Jesus, Elijah returned to the earth as John the Baptist, as planned, but unlike those saints he came to the earth through the womb of the Prophetess Elizabeth and, Zechariah being his new earthly father.

When John the Baptist was beheaded by Herod, John the Baptist (Elijah) returned to paradise. Jesus provided evidence of the prophet's return to paradise in a vision He showed to Peter, James and John at the Mount of Transfiguration:

"Now after six days Jesus took Peter, James, and John his brother, led them up on a high mountain by themselves; and He was transfigured before them.

His face shone like the sun, and His clothes became as white as the light. And behold, Moses and Elijah appeared to them, talking with Him.

Then Peter answered and said to Jesus, "Lord, it is good for us to be here; if you wish, let us make here three tabernacles: one for you, one for Moses, and one for Elijah." (Mathew 17:1-4).

First, this mountain has been suggested to be Mount Hermon.

They were airlifted spiritually by pilot Jesus taking them on the adventure

Let's take a cursory look at this mountain. Mount Hermon is about 9,232 feet high in elevation and 5,919 feet in prominence. Let me put this in modern day context. The mountain is about 9 times higher than the Eiffel Tower in France.

And there is no evidence from the scriptures that Peter, James and John and even the Lord Jesus, trained as mountain climbers. Nor were they carrying mountain climbing equipment in the context of this particular scripture. So the only way all four "went up" this high mountain is if they were airlifted.

Peter, James and John visited paradise, the third heaven, at the Mount of Transfiguration.

And yes, they were airlifted spiritually by pilot Jesus taking them on the adventure. Second, Peter's desire to make the mountain top his permanent residence is a cause for curiosity. Usually, mountain climbers are thrilled to reach the peak of a mountain after a lengthy ascent. But this is quickly short-lived by the desire to resume a descent, partly to share the good news and celebrate their great feat. And partly to get away from the mountain and return home to refresh. For a lay climber, you can imagine that staying at the peak of a high mountain like this without support railings will only last for as long as it takes them to eventually self-diagnose as acrophobic- the fear of height.

So it was not the thrill of being on the mountain top that sparked Peter's desire to live on the mountain. And it was not the sight of Elijah and Moses either. He said "Lord it is good for us to be here".

It was the surrounding. It is the "here" that enticed Peter. He then offered a way to get his desire fulfilled: "let us make a tabernacle for you, Moses and Elijah". All of Peter's senses grabbed the air of the 3rd heaven- paradise.

CHAPTER 8 – IS PARADISE ADJACENT TO HELL?

Let's look at the scriptures to see if paradise is adjacent to hell or Hades. First, the prophet Isaiah speaking through the Holy Spirit indicates that paradise is only a window away from Hades. Speaking about the righteous people who worship God in paradise and are able to see those suffering in hell:

> *"And they shall go forth and look upon the corpses of the men Who have transgressed against Me.*
>
> *For their worm does not die, and their fire is not quenched. They shall be abhorrence to all flesh." (Isaiah 66:24)*

Second, with the arrival of the Holy Spirit at Pentecost, the apostle Peter explains to the onlookers that the Holy Spirit was speaking about Jesus through David in the psalms:

"For you will not leave my soul in Hades, Nor will You allow Your Holy One to see corruption. You have made known to me the ways of life; you will make me full of joy in Your presence" (Acts 2:27-28)

David died and his flesh decayed in the grave. His soul did not go to Hades. He went to paradise because he was a righteous king who pleased God. As I have explained before about other righteous residents of paradise, David did not go to the presence of God in the Kingdom of God.

Clearly, as Peter explains to these onlookers, though it was David speaking, it was actually Jesus speaking about Himself through the Holy Spirit in David. Peter in this scripture confirms that Jesus went to Hades as soon as He died.

When Jesus went to Hades from the Cross, He was for the first time in eternity past, present and future, separated from God the Father. He had to go to Hades where death, a spirit, lives, and where there is total separation from God.

This is important for you and I. Jesus went to Hades to face death (a spirit), with His blood that He shed, in order to seal our redemption so we don't have to go there. The bible says that the wages of sin is death. Death is not just the physical death. It is also a spiritual and eternal death.

So Jesus went to face this Satan's spirit, called death in Hades, to pay the wages for sin on our behalf so we do not have to go there. This required separation from God the Father because the punishment for sin required a complete separation from God.

And since Jesus has chosen to bear this costly consequence of sin on our behalf, He had to be separated from His Father God, with whom He had existed in trinity with the Holy Spirit. God the Son separated Himself from

God the Father. In other words, God separated Himself from God.

This is very significant and calls for sober reflection. On the Cross, Jesus did not lament "my father, my father, why have you forsaken me" just because of what He suffered from the hands of sinful created beings or because He faced death. No, He lamented more because He knew of this painful separation from God that He Has willingly volunteered Himself to do on our behalf.

Watch this, the bible did not tell us how God the Father handled this situation in heaven where His Only begotten Son with whom He existed for as long as He existed, hung on the Cross and was about to be separated from Him for the first time. It was the breaking of the trinity triangle as I God reveals Himself later in this book.

We were made in God's image and in His likeness; we carry the different types of emotions to respond to different situations. Likewise, the bible is full of evidences of God demonstrating different types of emotions at different times.

Then you and I cannot be too off if we imagine that just before this unusual separation between the father and his son, the angels surround the creator God to console Him.

Yes, because Jesus was sad for the situation, you can imagine the Father in heaven feeling the same way. God has given His best and it cost Him His best. If you or anyone around you has not received Jesus, God's best gift to humanity, it is about time we do so. It is about time we tell others about this profound sacrifice of Jesus, by God and for all of mankind.

So, in the scripture above, it was Jesus speaking to God the Father during the planning phase of His journey to earth for our redemption. David was allowed to listen in on their conversation through the Holy Spirit.

In that deliberation, Jesus, (God the Son), reaffirms His trust in God the Father that the Father would *"not leave my soul in Hades, Nor will You allow [the flesh] of Your Holy One to see corruption".*

Jesus' body did not decay in the grave as He rose from it the third day. And His soul did not remain in Hades as God already showed Him the ways for life to paradise from where He went to the presence of God in the heavenly Kingdom of God.

Third, our good Lord Jesus Has answers to this important question. The story He gives below is not a parable. It is a revelation, an eye witness account of where He Himself has been to and what He Has seen:

"There was a certain rich man who was clothed in purple and fine linen and fared sumptuously every day.

But there was a certain beggar named Lazarus, full of sores, who was laid at his gate, desiring to be fed with the crumbs which fell from the rich man's table. Moreover the dogs came and licked his sores.

So it was that the beggar died, and was carried by the angels to Abraham's bosom. The rich man also died and was buried.

And being in torments in Hades, he lifted up his eyes and saw Abraham afar off, and Lazarus in his bosom. (Luke 16:19-23)

Let's unpack this eye witness account given by Jesus together. There are two destinations – one is Abraham's bosom for the righteous, and Hades for the unrighteous. Being poor or being rich did not qualify anyone of the two for the destination they went to.

After all, Abraham himself was one of the richest people of his generation but the rich man in this case did not make the cut to his bosom. Evidence of the rich man's unrighteousness or wickedness can be seen in the way he treated the poor Lazarus.

Likewise, Lazarus did not qualify for Abraham's bosom just because of his suffering on earth. He was qualified for the bosom because there is no reference in this scripture that he acted wickedly, hence only the rich man was left to Hades.

Notice that Lazarus was carried by angels. Angels report to Jesus. So, it was on the instruction of Jesus. And here is the bottom line: Abraham's bosom is paradise, the 3rd heaven, a temporary heaven where the righteous reside until Jesus returns for all the righteous for their final flight into the heavenly kingdom of God – the 4th heaven.

Therefore, Abraham, Isaac and Jacob, Moses and Elijah, Noah, are all eagerly waiting for the final flight. Why shouldn't you? Remember my reference to the episode between Nicodemus and Jesus in John 3. Jesus said to him:

> *"[...] Most assuredly, I say to you, unless one is born again, he cannot see the kingdom of God."(John 3:3).*

> *"[...] Most assuredly, I say to you, unless one is born of water and the Spirit, he cannot enter the kingdom of God" (John 3:5).*

Yes, the righteousness and good deeds of the old testament saints were accepted by God and computed as righteousness because Jesus, the Lamb of God had been slain before the foundation of the world. This qualified them for paradise.

*Abraham, Moses and Elijah, Noah, are all
waiting for the final flight. Why shouldn't you?*

Transcendental Power of Jesus' Blood

The power of the blood Jesus physically shed on the cross is transcendental. It cleanses sin and rebellion both in the terrestrial (the seen) and celestial (the unseen) existences. First of all, Noah, Abraham, Isaac and all the righteous men of the Old Testament must be born again; must be born of water and of the Spirit, to enter the kingdom of God. And being born again happens through the sacrifice of the blood that Jesus shed on Calvary cross.

Jesus had made the sacrifice of blood long before He even came to the earth. That is why John the beloved refers to Jesus as the Lamb of God who was slain from the foundation of the world (Revelation 13:8).

It was not the blood of animals that earned forgiveness for people in the Old Testament. Each time they sacrificed animal blood, God remembered the blood of Jesus, the Lamb of God who was slain from the foundation of the world.

In other words, before they were ever created, our omniscient Creator God knew that our first parents Adam and Eve would fall into Sin, hence He had made a provision for the redemption of all of mankind. The footprint of Jesus the redeeming Lamb of God was all over the Old Testament.

When God began the plan to send Jesus to demonstrate in the physical realm, the sacrifice of blood Jesus had made in the realm of the spirit before we were made, He began the plan with Father Abraham. The bible says in the book of Genesis that Abraham believed God and it was credited to him as righteousness.

Now it is important to note that Abraham obtained just righteousness because he believed God. Not salvation. Salvation came to him when he met with Jesus the King of Righteousness Himself. He met with Melchizedek who was a type of Christ (Genesis 14).

This further demonstrates that Jesus has had His footprint on the earth in the Old Testament making preparation for the ultimate sacrifice He would make on Calvary Cross later in the New Testament.

Melchizedek, the "King of Peace," of "Righteousness" and the Priest of God Most High, gave Abraham bread and wine. Abraham in return gave Melchizedek a tenth of all the spoils he got from a recent victory in battles with the Kings.

Here is one insight on this episode with the King of Righteousness. With the bread and wine Abraham took from Him, Jesus imputed His body and blood into Abraham and subsequently to his seed Isaac and all of Abraham's descendants, including those with genealogical link to Isaac and to Joseph and Mary, the earthly parents of Jesus.

When Abraham gave Jesus-Melchizedek a tenth of his battle spoils, he was indicating that he surrendered Himself completely to Melchizedek as his king, his Lord and Savior. Abraham became born again at this point.

Isaac is the promised seed for redemption where the earthly genealogy of Jesus Christ began. That's why the psalmist, speaking through the Holy Spirit, says about Jesus: *"The Lord has sworn and will not relent, "You are a priest forever according to the order of Melchizedek."(Psalm 110:4).* See how the preacher man in the bible describes Melchizedek as Jesus:

> *"For this Melchizedek, king of Salem, priest of the Most High God, who met Abraham returning from the slaughter of the kings and blessed him, to whom also*

> *Abraham gave a tenth part of all, first being translated "king of righteousness," and then also king of Salem, meaning "king of peace," without father,*
>
> *without mother, without genealogy, having neither beginning of days nor end of life, but made like the Son of God, remains a priest continually"(Hebrews 7:1-3).*

Jesus the slain Lamb of God performed the sacrifice for our redemption from sin before the foundation of the world. He made a footprint on the earth in the Old Testament through Melchizedek to continue this work of redemption. Every time in the Old Testament, the blood of animals was sprinkled on sinners for the forgiveness of sin.

Each time this sacrifice was made, it was the blood of Jesus the slain Lamb of God from the foundation of the world that made the sacrifices of the blood of animals acceptable to God.

Jesus was finally conceived of the Holy Spirit in the New Testament and came to the earth through a virgin birth after which He proceeded to Calvary cross to do what He had done from the foundation of the world.

After His resurrection, He sits on the right side of the throne of God where he currently makes intercession for His believers. He also travels back and forth between His throne in the Kingdom of God (the 4th heaven) and paradise, the 3rd heaven.

Paradise, as explained before, is like Jesus' summer village, where He spends time with Abraham, Lazarus and all His righteous people who are now born again, born of water and of the Spirit because of Jesus. They are the old flock that must be brought together with the new flock in the New Testament for the final flight.

Although residents of paradise currently sometimes visit the Kingdom of God as spirit and soulish beings escorted by Jesus or His angels, they will enter the kingdom of God with their resurrected, glorified body when Jesus comes for the final flight of all the saints of God.

Notice this: at the time Jesus made the statement to Nicodemus in the bible that no one has entered heaven (the kingdom), these residents of paradise could not visit the kingdom of God.

But after Jesus went to the Cross, shed His blood and rose from the dead, the veil of the temple of God has been torn, granting direct access to the presence of God in the Kingdom through Jesus.

Therefore, Jesus remains what He called Himself- "[...] I am the way, the truth and the life. No one comes to the Father except by me" (John 14:6). And to enter the Kingdom of God, we must accept Him and Him alone as Lord and saviour.

As I mentioned at the beginning of this book, Jesus does not only take His saints from paradise to the throne of God in the 4th heaven, He also takes His saints who are alive on the earth for this visit.

Evangelist Mary Baxter was taken by Jesus and escorted by an angel to Hell for 30 days and to heaven for 10 days. In her bestseller book, *A Divine Revelation of Heaven*, she recounts how she was transported:

> *"On the thirty-first night after these events began, the power of Almighty God fell on me again. At two o'clock in the morning, a mighty angel stood beside my bed.*
>
> *Jesus Christ was standing behind the angel. As I looked on the face of the Lord standing*

there, He smiled at me, but He did not say anything.

The mighty messenger of God said, "God has given me a special mission. I am sent here to take you to heaven and to show you parts of it."

After a moment, he spoke again, "Come and see the glory of God!" At once, I was supernaturally transported from my home and found myself standing outside one of the gates of heaven with the heavenly angel" (Baxter, Mary p.16-17)

Looking intently at Baxter's experience both to hell and heaven, it appears that with this great woman of God, Jesus intends only to focus our attention on the destinations – heaven and hell.

She was transported from her home and immediately found herself standing outside one of the gates of heaven with the heavenly angel.

There is less emphasis on how she got there. I encourage you to read her books as Jesus has a lot to show to the world in them. On the contrary, through my own repeated experience as described in this book, the Lord's intent is to paint a vivid picture of the final journey to the kingdom of God.

Jesus wants you to believe in this soon-to happen glorious event. Not only that, He wants everyone who has not turned to Him as Lord, to look at this promise and do so.

I have seen Jesus several times

I have seen Jesus several times in dream-visions. About three times He appeared suspended in the sky as though descended for the final flight of believers. Each time He did this, as though to assure me He was the one, He descended further only to show me the nail marks on His hands and legs from the wound He sustained when He was nailed to the Cross.

At another instance, I saw Jesus in a dream-vision come swiftly to my rescue when falling down the cliff. Still another time, on July 7, 2014, the day after I preached a message titled "The Divine Purpose and Favor" at a church, Jesus appeared to me again.

I had preached that an evangelistic focus on the divine purpose of all believers is the expansion of the kingdom of God. I had mentioned in the message that a focus on this divine purpose attracts divine favour and blessing from God. I had explained and demonstrated that almost every instance of favour in the bible is intricately linked to this divine favour.

So, Jesus appeared to me the next morning. He showed me a piece of diamond with thumbs up to me indicating His approval of the message I preached the day before.

We were planning for the Canada Walk 4 Jesus parade in Edmonton. On April 7, 2017, Jesus came to me again in a dream-vision.

In the vision, I climbed and came off the escalator where I sometimes handed out gospel cards at the Century Park train station in Edmonton. As soon as I got to the top of the escalator, Jesus appeared to me and here is what He said:

> *"A report came to me that you are slowing down. I know you are planning some events (*referring to the Canada Walk 4 Jesus parade in Edmonton*). Work hard at it and I will bring you to God's eternal kingdom".*

I woke up from this knowing that the Lord is not done with me as confirmed in a word of knowledge by several other ministers. I have had angels appear and spoken to me as well.

Whatever else Jesus reveals to me, I will be sure to proclaim it on the roof as best as I can. Jesus reveals to redeem. The sole purpose of any divine revelation is the redemption of precious souls to God.

The Holy Spirit woke me up. He gave me some very profound revelations of the triangle shape

CHAPTER 9– LIFE TRIANGLE- HOLY TRINITY EXPLAINED

As we focus on the coming of Jesus and the final flight with Him, it is important to know about who we will be travelling with and His relationship with the God-Head, the Holy Trinity – God the Father, God the Son and God the Holy Spirit.

There is one God and He exists in three forms. These three forms of the same one God have journeyed to the earth fulfilling purpose for mankind in an ordered, coordinated, scheduled, and interdependent manner.

On November 1, 2017 at exactly 2:00am, the Holy Spirit woke me up. He gave me some very profound revelations of the triangle shape. He impressed on me that God had allowed the invention of the triangle to use to explain His trinity identity to the world and His journey to and from the earth.

I will explain to you what precious Holy Spirit impressed on me about the triangle shape that early morning. You already know that the triangle is the only shape with three equal sides and angles.

The triangle will guide us to understand the God that exists in three forms (trinity) – God the father, God the Son and God the Holy Spirit.

The triangle remains one triangle despite its three angles that are connected with each other. It is the same with God. He remains one God despite His three equal sides and angles that are also connected with each other.

Before creating time and space, God knew the task ahead of Him and He wanted a connected team that is not part of creation. That team had to be He Himself. Hence, He replicates into three equal angles to fit His design of the creative order.

So, the triangle existed before you. That's why the book of the beginnings (genesis) in the bible identifies this trinity team. God the Father spoke the word (which is His son), one of the three equal angles. His Holy Spirit, another angle, hovered over a formless earth. The book of John also accounts for this creative team.

The reason for this replication is that at every point in time in all of existence, God desires to have His presence with all of His creation.

This way, the triangle team can navigate the unseen heavens and the seen earth at the same time. The one God that is in three forms can travel back and forth the universe and make anywhere His creation is, a dwelling place as He pleases.

That's why after creating the visible world, He said to His trinity triangle team in Genesis 2 of the bible, *"let us make man in our own image and our likeness"*. So, the human is manufactured along the design of God Himself.

That's why the human race is in trinity too. We are first spirit-beings, we have a soul and we live in a body. Our spirit connects us to God. Our soul connects us to ourselves. And our body is the earthly tent that connects us to the world we live in and other creations in it. Like God, you are a triangular being!

Like the triangle God, Adam and Eve existed both in the visible and the invisible existence of created universe. Their city was the beautiful Garden of Eden, a spiritual existence. Then sin came into these first humans through disobedience to the Creator God.

As the Creator has prerogative over His creation, He threw them out of the Garden of Eden and their ability to have their dwelling both in the visible and the invisible realm of creation like the triangle God, ceased.

Man died and became limited to the visible existence – the uncultivated earth. Therefore, as the bible says, since we came from Adam and Eve, all of mankind have sinned and have lost the glory of God they had before the fall of mankind.

It was the glory that enabled mankind to traverse the visible and invisible realms of creation like the triangle God. This was done not without the life triangle again.

With the triangle, God the Father is on top of the angle facing up while the son and the Holy Spirit are on the angles pointing down, suggesting the father is head over the trinity triangle. And that's because the Son and the Holy Spirit are on a mission on earth.

Jesus, one of the equal angles of God, came from heaven to earth to shed His blood and die as payment for the punishment of death that comes as a result of sin. When Jesus came, He died on the cross – an open triangle with a long tail is formed as you will see with the shape of the Cross.

The sides of this triangle are not connected or linked to each other because Jesus alone came and the third angle, the Holy Spirit only breathes into Him. That's why you have the long line across the Cross triangle.

The long tail of this cross points to the earth from which man was made. With the long tail, Jesus followed mankind to its fallen state under the earth when He died.

Jesus rose from the dead and walked on earth to the right of the triangle and goes back up into heaven where He came from. Mankind has to approach the cross from the earth. All of mankind. They have to walk on Jesus' path and someday be called upon to come up to where Jesus is in the heavenly kingdom.

Rotating Trinity Triangle

With the triangle, God the Father is on top of the angle facing up while the Son and the Holy Spirit are on the angles pointing down, suggesting the father is head over the trinity triangle. And that's because the Son and the Holy Spirit are on a mission on earth.

When you flip the other angles of the triangle one by one, you will see the son or the Holy Spirit on top, indicating different leads over the trinity.

When the triangle is completely upside down, one of the three equals is on earth while the other two are in heaven.

When God the Father was revealing Himself through His Spirit that came upon Old Testament prophets, God the Son and God the Holy Spirit were not revealed. They were in heaven.

The triangle is flipped when God the Son came through Jesus in the New Testament. The other two equal angles - the Father and the Holy Spirit concealed their identity in heaven.

The triangle is flipped again when God the Holy Spirit revealed Himself in this church age, God the Son and the Father are in heaven.

So at every time any one of the three equal angles of the triangle-God comes to the earthly realm, the triangle must be upside down, with one angle reaching the earth and the other two in heaven.

When the triangle is upside down, one of the three angles or the trinity is on earth. That's why when it comes to His business on earth; God does things in reverse order. He uses the foolish things of this world to confound the wise. He wants the crooked Jacob over Esau, David over His brothers, young Joseph over his eldest siblings, Ephraim over Manasseh etc.

God has inscribed the triangle, the creative design of His trinity on the Shield of David

God has inscribed His creative design on many of creations without us knowing this. Do you know the Jewish national symbol? It is the shield of King David also known as the Star of David. Guess what? When you unpack the Star of David, you will realize that it is two triangles combined, one facing up, the other facing down.

This is a mystery revealed to me by the Holy Spirit. God completes the revelation of His identity in the Shield of David. The upright triangle describes the three equals before they began the team work for creation.

The triangle upside down placed on the one standing upright in this David's shield, demonstrates that the three equals have come to earth on a missionary journey, one at a time. They have come for creation, redemption and finally, they will come for the restoration of everything back to God in the final flight. This is the Life Triangle!

For restoration of all created saints, the image of the triangle also comes into play with the coming appearance of Jesus in the sky when He returns for His believers.

As the scripture says, the Lord Himself will descend with a loud shout, with the voice of the archangel and with the trumpet call of God. It is the same, equal Lord. But He must manifest in three equal ways for three different purposes.

Rotating Triangle – The Trinity Team

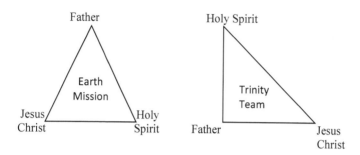

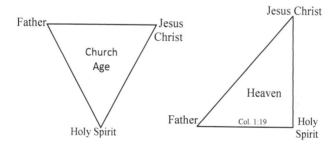

Trinity Before Creation

Trinity After creation

CHAPTER 10 – THE SECOND HEAVEN - HADES

Early Sunday morning in March 2018, I had just finished praying and reading the scriptures. I lay on the couch in my prayer room to rest. I was awake when suddenly Jesus opened my eyes in an open vision to see Satan's command and control centre in the air. I call this command and control centre the second heaven and its inner extension is Hades.

In the context of the bible, the heavens or the heavenlies include the skies above the earth, the human navigated and known planetary system (the 1st heaven), the restricted spiritual existence of Hades which is an extension of the kingdom of the air (the 2nd heaven).

The heavens include paradise, Abraham's Bosom or reoccupied Garden of Eden (the 3rd heaven), and the heavenly kingdom of God, where God dwells (the 4th heaven). Look at the open vision shared by the apostle Paul that someone else saw in the bible:

> *It is doubtless not profitable for me to boast. I will come to visions and revelations of the Lord: I know a man in Christ who fourteen years ago—*

*whether in the body I do not know, or
whether out of the body I do not know,*

*God knows—such a one was caught up to
the third heaven. And I know such a man—
whether in the body or out of the body I do
not know,*

*God knows—how he was caught up into
Paradise and heard inexpressible words,
which it is not lawful for a man to utter."*

In this scripture, Paul retells the story of a man who was
taken up to paradise. He also indicated that this third
heaven is paradise.

This means there is a first and second heaven and since I
have indicated in this book that paradise is the Garden of
Eden and a temporary place, there must be a 4th heaven- the
Kingdom of God.

The first heaven is the atmosphere known to those who
dwelled on the earth in the bible age and later known as the
planetary system in modern church age where humans have
now navigated. The second heaven is the kingdom of the
air- a spiritual existence, as I explain further in this chapter.

This second heaven is Satan's command and control
centre in the air and it has an inner extension –Hades or
hell. The third heaven is paradise, as mentioned in the
scriptures above or the Garden of Eden or Abraham's
bosom.

The 4th heaven is of course the heavenly kingdom of
God – the destination for the final flight of all saints when
Jesus returns.

In the open vision that Sunday morning, I saw Satan
from afar off suspended in the air and below him were
multiple piles of mountains. The site I saw was

convincingly a place right on top of the earthly realm. He was suspended in the air.

In that moment, the Holy Spirit told me this: "that is the Prince of the Kingdom of the Air as Paul describes him in Ephesians 2". Satan or the Prince of the air, was giving marching orders to other princes (principalities) assigned to different continents and countries of the world.

Jesus impressed on me that the Prince of the kingdom of the air just instructed his princes to go out and cause people in government to begin to make decisions that are ungodly and unreasonable.

Satan, the Prince instructed other princes to go to churches and cause disunity and confusion and into homes to cause commotion and to governments, so they take unreasonable actions.

A few moments later, I saw a snake around a people in turmoil and conflict but they did not see it. I was pointing to them to see the snake and keep a distance from it to be safe, they could not hear as they were deep into a fight.

The Prince of the Kingdom of the Air, Satan, had been forced into his current territory when he became a fallen angel because of his rebellion towards God and after he lost the cosmic battle in the heavenly kingdom of God (the 4th heaven).

John the Beloved describes Satan's exit from heaven when he was thrown to the earth (Revelation 12). The earth in this context is the lower part of the heavens that is within the atmospheric layout of the earth.

The Holy Spirit told me this: "that is the Prince of the Kingdom of the Air as Paul describes him in Ephesians 2."

As I stated earlier, the second heaven is the existence beyond the atmospheric geography where human space exploration has navigated. Satan rules the world from here as the Prince of the kingdom of the Air. An extension of this Satan's command and control centre in the air is Hades, also known as hell, a place of death, a temporary place of torment for those who do not have the redeeming blood of Jesus over them.

Writing to the Ephesian church and referring to Jesus' death, His visit to hell and His eventual ascension into heaven, the apostle Paul says:

> *"(Now this "He ascended"- what does it mean but that He also first descended into the lower parts of the earth?*
>
> *He who descended is also the One who ascended far above all the heavens, that He might fill all things.)" (Ephesians 4:9-10).*

The lower parts of the earth in this case are the kingdom of the air and its inner extension, hell. Demons live in hell from where they visit the earth as spirit beings to unleash Satan's horror of sin, disobedience, sickness, bondage and oppression on humankind.

In addition to the open vision the Lord showed me with Satan standing at his command and control centre in the kingdom of the air, I have seen him appear to me to challenge me on two other occasions.

The first time he came, he came like an angel of light. During the desert or valley experience that I described earlier, I felt the need to encourage myself in the Lord as David in the bible had to do. I lay in my guest room.

I picked up my diary and I was reading out the promises God has made to me. As I began reading them out, I was getting encouraged.

And a bit of excitement came with it given that they were made by Jesus, a promise-maker that always keeps to His promises and that Has the power to fulfill them.

Suddenly, Satan appeared to me, suspended in the air. He appeared to be trying to hide his face so I don't recognize it was him speaking to me. He instead turned his back at me and he began to speak.

He appeared to agree that the promises will be fulfilled. And then he says: "but they won't last long." I immediately rebuked him. I said "Satan, the Lord rebuke you". They will last long and I will last long. I don't recall what I said to him next.

I probably must have said "I resist you in the name of Jesus". And then he vanished. The second time, I was in my prayer room. After praying, I was sleeping off, Satan appeared as the evil force that he is on the wall of the room. He tried to overpower me with a thunderous echoing voice.

I managed to get up and my spirit continued rebuking him in Jesus name till I woke up. Don't engage him in a fight. He is a powerful being because God gave him the power when he was still under God as an angel.

Satan is so powerful to the point that the bible records that even God's general, the archangel Michael, had to wrestle with him in the battle for custody of Moses' body. But if Satan comes at you, and you are born again, know for sure that he sees Jesus in you when you mention Jesus' name.

As powerful as he and his demons may appear, when you mention the name of Jesus, they must flee. "For greater is He that is in you than he that is in the world". The Lord has in the past shown me Satan's prince, the principality responsible for Canada. Canada's prince (principality), was a very tall giant, as high as an electric pole and he was suspended in the air. He represents Satan, the prince of the kingdom of the air in Canada.

When I finished serving the party line and turned back to leave, I was only about 20 feet away when I sensed in my spirit the urge to look back.

There was another day I saw one of Satan's demonic spirits appear to me in the physical. I lay on the couch sleeping. Somehow, it felt like I was being strangled and I struggled to free myself and I broke free, waking up.

As I opened my eyes, the demon was like a lady standing at the other end of the couch and probably was unaware that I was now awake. As soon as I wanted to start saying something in Jesus name, she disappeared.

I am sharing all these with you so you can tangibly see that darkness is as tangible as light. And whether or not we like it, anyone that doesn't make it to the flight with Jesus has chosen the other part of darkness that leads to perdition.

I recall one of those nights I went to Whyte Avenue, a notorious party street in Edmonton City in Canada. Young adults were lined up in a freezing weather to enter a club for all forms of sinful acts – drunkenness, lasciviousness, drug and alcoholic abuse, nakedness, all forms of sexual immorality.

As I handed out gospel cards to the party goers, I spotted two girls among them that were uniquely different in their distinctively half nakedness and make-up. One of the two pretended to be drunk. For some reason, my spirit was quick to know that it was a pretence. She was not drunk.

Standing by each other, her companion asks dismissively about the cards I was handing out, "is that God?" as though not trying to call the name of Jesus. They of course refused to collect the card unlike the rest of the precious souls on the party lines.

I finished serving the party line and turned back to leave, I was only about 20 feet away when I sensed in my spirit the urge to look back.

As I did, the two girls were gazing at me as if they were hoping I leave. Their faces glowed in the dark. Their eyes flashed as you would see a red laser light penetrating to hit its focused target. At that point, I knew they were not humans. They were demons sent from the pit of Hades.

They were on assignment to influence sinful behaviours among the unsuspecting young adults and adults. I walked on to tell my fellow street preachers what I had just seen. On reaching the podium upon which one of them was standing and preaching, I saw the girl that was pretending to be drunk coming from the opposite direction towards us.

The only way someone I just left behind me could be approaching me from the opposite direction is if they disappeared from the back to appear in front of me. So the demon pretending to be a drunken girl walked in between the street preacher on the podium and someone trying to heckle him.

When she walked past, still pretending to be drunk, she gave me a stare as though she was boastfully telling me that hell had a firm grip on the lost souls on the Whyte and there was no way of letting them loose.

I am sharing this with you my friend not to scare you. But to show you that Hades and the residents living in it, including demons who are able to visit the earth, are as tangible as day and night. They work hard on Satan's marching orders to limit the number of people that will qualify to go in the final flight when Jesus comes.

CHAPTER 11 – WHERE ARE THE SINFUL DEAD?

The sinful dead are in Hades, also called hell. Satan and his demons are in Hades, though they are able to traverse the earth. So is everyone that died in their sins without the forgiveness that comes only through the redeeming blood of Jesus.

That includes people in the Old and the New Testaments of the bible. As I explained to you earlier, people in the Old Testament that escaped from being thrown into Hades when they died had been washed with the blood of Jesus through faith and obedience to God's instructions.

Each time they slaughtered animals in sacrifice to God, they invoked the redeeming blood of Jesus the Lamb of God who was slain from the foundation of the world. God accepted Abraham's faith for righteousness because the Lamb of God had made it possible with His blood.

As hinted briefly the previous chapters, I want to point to you a more profound impact of this innocent blood. Its redeeming power spans across existence before creation in genesis. Satan's original rebellion in heaven which he later transferred to mankind at the Garden of Eden did not only taint the human species and separated us from God.

The rebellion tainted all of God's creations including prior orders of creation - angels, the 24 elders and the 4 living creatures sitting by God's throne in heaven, as John the Beloved reveals in Revelation. The blood of Jesus, the Lamb of God was needed to redeem from the original sin of rebellion and reconcile even angels, the 24 elders and the 4 living creatures back to God.

This is a mystery-truth and God would have us engrave into our hearts about the precious blood of Jesus. In the vision Jesus gave to John, a scroll in the hands of God was to be opened.

No one in heaven or on earth was qualified to open the scroll. When John was worried and wept because no one was able to open the scroll, one of the elders said to him:

> *"Do not weep. Behold, the Lion of the tribe of Judah, the Root of David, has prevailed to open the scroll and to loose its seven seals.(Revelation 5:4).* Look at what John saw afterwards:

> *"And I looked, and behold, in the midst of the throne and of the four living creatures, and in the midst of the elders, stood a Lamb as though it had been slain,*

> *having seven horns and seven eyes, which the seven Spirits of God are sent out into all the earth. Then He came and took the scroll out of the right hand of Him who sat on the throne (Revelation 5:6-7).*

Now see what Jesus reveals to John the Beloved about the all-encompassing power of redemption that is contained in His blood. See the testimony given about the blood when the 24 elders and the 4 living creatures bowed down to worship Jesus the Lamb of God:

> *"And they [the 4 living creatures and the 24 elders] sang a new song, saying: You are worthy to take the scroll, And to open its seals;*
>
> *For You were slain, And have redeemed us to God by Your blood out of every tribe and tongue and people and nation, And have made us kings and priests to our God; And we shall reign on the earth (Revelation 5:10."*

Can you see The 24 elders thanking Jesus for redeeming them?! Can you see the 4 living creatures who are not in the creative order of human beings and who sit in the closest proximity to the throne of God, thanking Jesus the Lamb of God for His blood which He shed for their redemption?!

Can you see them praise and worship Jesus the Lamb of God for redeeming them to God by His blood: *"For you were slain, And have redeemed us to God by Your blood out of every tribe and tongue [...] (Revelation 5:9).*

Now pay attention to this revelation. What is known is that Satan deceived a third of the angels in heaven to follow him (according to the book of revelation), who are now demons destined together with him for eternal ruin in the Lake of Fire, the final home for God's enemies.

In actual fact, he deceived more than a third of the angels and other orders of creation before humans as the scripture reveals about the 4 living creatures. Only a third of those he deceived fell flat for his deception and were eventually banished with him from the 4th heaven to the earth. The remaining creations took advantage of the shed blood of the Lamb for their redemption from the sin of rebellion.

Therefore, the next time you see people say there are multiple ways to the creator God, tell them even the angels needed to be cleansed by the blood of Jesus to be with God.

These heavenly beings appreciate Jesus for what He has done. In just the same way like the creations in heaven, the blood of the Lamb is available for our redemption to God. Only those who take this blood by turning to Jesus are saved.

Others will remain in disobedience and they will be banished from the presence of God forever, just like the angels that refused to repent were banished from heaven. There is no salvation through any religion of the world. No other religion has claimed to deal with the problem of sin. Only Jesus did.

The blood of Jesus the Lamb of God was needed to redeem from the original sin of rebellion and reconcile even angels, the 24 elders and the 4 living creatures back to God.

Therefore, I echo Apostle Paul's conviction and injunction to us: If the Archbishop, the Pope, pastor, evangelist, healing miracle worker or an angel suggests to you that there are multiple ways to God, that Jesus is not the only way to redemption from sin and reconciliation with God, let them be eternally condemned!

They are either ravenous wolves in sheep's clothing or they too have become victims of ravenous wolves. As Jude instructs, if you can, save them from the coming fire by sharing the unassailable truth of Jesus with them. If not, run from them, faster than a moving vehicle.

Their message is from Hades and you do not need to go there because Jesus went on your behalf. Peter talks about Jesus to the rulers, elders, the scribes and the high priest (the Jews in Jerusalem):

> *This is the 'stone which was rejected by you builders, which has become the chief cornerstone.'*
>
> *Nor is there salvation in any other, for there is no other name under heaven given among men by which we must be saved."(Acts 4:11-12.*

Everyone who rejects Jesus is rejecting the only provision God has made to deal with their sins.

Because of the Sin of disobedience, rebellion, Adam and Eve allowed Satan to input into them at the beautiful Garden of Eden.

All of the humankind descended from these first earthly parents, hence as the bible says, we have all sinned and have come short of the glory of God.

The tainted creations in heaven could not remain with the Holy God and were banished to earth, Hades, or the second heaven. In the same way, anyone who refuses to be cleansed by the blood of Jesus will also end up in Hades when they die.

All the rebellious creations will eventually be brought for judgment and be thrown into the Lake of Fire that will burn without end.

This is not what God wants for you and me. This destination was designed for Satan and the fallen angels. Unfortunately, the seed of their rebellion manifested in sin cannot be carried into the presence of God.

Even the angels needed to be cleansed by the blood of Jesus to be with God

Sin must be dealt with by the blood of Jesus. If not, Satan will have a legal right to claim humans that still have his seed of sin and rebellion for his eternal place of endless suffering, first, in Hades, and later, in the Lake of Fire.

As John records in the book of revelation, death, Hades, Satan, the demons and all disobedient people will eventually be cast into the Lake of Fire (Revelation 20:14).

The word Hades or hell occurs about 11 times in the New Testament, 5 of which is Jesus directly mentioning it and the remaining 6 times were said by the apostles inspired by Him (Acts 2:27, 2:31, Luke 10:15,16:23, Mathew 11:23, 16:18, 1 Corinthians 15:55, Revelation 1:18, 6:8, 20:13-14). There is no denying that Hades or hell exists as some are in the habit of doing.

So when you see people who present themselves to represent God and Jesus denying there is no place called Hell, they are either a victim of deceit by the devil or are themselves the perpetrators of evil lies. I want you to show them these scriptures and pray that the veil of darkness over them be removed by the precious Holy Spirit.

Where they are perpetrators of this evil lies, I want you to warn them in love of the danger ahead of them for their informed contribution to heresy that deceives sinners. Many reject the gospel of Jesus assuming there is no consequence for sin and they are lured into this eternal consequence.

Where any wolf in sheep's clothing refuses to listen, keep them at a distance. They want to steal eternity with God from you and lure you into Hades.

In her national best-selling book, *"A Divine Revelation of Hell – Time is Running Out"*, the Evangelist Mary K. Baxter, recounts her experience when Jesus took her in a repeated revelation journey to Hades for 30 days.

The horror of those who died in their sins and now in Hell cannot be described in words. But she gave a profound depiction of what Jesus showed her to tell the world about hell.

I recommend that you obtain all of Baxter's books to read. They will lift your faith and get you ready for the coming of the Lord Jesus and the final flight of His saints. In one of her accounts of "The Left Leg of Hell", Baxter recounts the monologue of a woman who so bitterly regrets she did not follow Jesus. See a part of the woman's monologue when she saw Jesus during the visit to Hell:

> *"Satan used my beauty and my money, and all my thoughts turned to how much power he would give me. Even then, God continued to draw me. But I thought, I have tomorrow or the next day.*
>
> *Then one day while riding in a car, my driver ran into a house, and I was killed. Lord, please let me out.' As she spoke, her bony hands and arms reached out to Jesus while the flames continued to burn her.*
>
> *Jesus said, 'The judgment is set' Tears fell down His cheeks as we moved to the next pit. I was crying inside about the horrors of hell. "Dear Lord," I cried, "the torment is too real.*
>
> *When a soul comes here, there is no hope, no life, no love. 'Hell is too real.' No way out, I thought. She must burn forever in these flames" (pp. 33-34)*

So our compassionate Jesus still wept for those in hell. Unfortunately, His grace is no longer available to save, as "the judgment is set".

The bible says it is appointed for mankind to die once, after death is judgment. My good friend, if at this point you have not been washed of the blood of Jesus, I urge you to ask God for forgiveness now.

Ask Him to use the blood of Jesus to wash your sins and tell Jesus you want to make Him your Lord and Savior. You see, the grace of Jesus is like an ocean for you now. Why not dive in?

As with the case of this woman in the Left Leg of Hell, when death comes, grace is no longer available. So now is a good time to have Jesus as Lord and savior. He is the ticket to paradise and the passport to the heavenly Kingdom of God at the final flight of all the saints of God.

Baxter records Jesus' description of hell in a way that furthers my explanation of Hades and its location based on the scriptures and the revelations Jesus gave me:

> *"Jesus spoke again, "Hell has a body (like a human form) lying on her back in the center of the earth. Hell is shaped like a human body – very large and with many chambers of torment.*
>
> *Remember to tell the people of earth that hell is real. Millions of lost souls are here, and more are coming every day.*
>
> *On the Great Judgment Day, death and hell will be cast into the lake of fire; that will be the second death"*

CHAPTER 12 – A COMFORT MEDICINE

The word of God in the bible is like a pharmacy store. When you have the right prescription medicine, you will get well. Often times we use the wrong medicine for situations we face as Christians. The doctrine of the Coming of Jesus Christ and the Final Flight of His Saints is bible's strongest prescription medicine to give or receive comfort.

You will notice that the only time Paul's writing to the Thessalonians on the coming of the Lord is read in church or other Christian gatherings is at the funeral ceremony of someone who died.

This is understandable given the biblical context as Paul was responding to those who were in deep mourning of the death of their loved ones when He wrote the revelations in 1 Thessalonians 4.

However, this is a restrictive use of this scripture on comfort. The promise of the coming of Jesus and the final flight of His believers is bible's prescription for comfort, hope, endurance and encouragement in all situations.

When you are betrayed by fellow believers, lied upon, or persecuted by those who have not seen the light, look up and imagine Jesus in the sky and you travelling with billions of saintly people in the glorious flight to the glorious destination.

When you are sick in your body and the time for your healing is taking forever, imagine yourself travelling with your glorified body in the final flight and you will be comforted.

When in service of the Lord, there seems to be no help around you, those for whose sake you experience pain in turn cause you pain by their words and actions, and you are down, you look up and imagine your savior appear in the sky for His faithful servants. You will be comforted.

When you need to go for a comfort mission or to make a comfort call to anyone whether or not they are a believer and notwithstanding the situation, the hope for the coming of Jesus and the final flight is the prescription.

In the bible, Jacob was deceived that his beloved son Joseph had been killed by a wild animal. Joseph had been sold to slavery in Egypt. But that was the end of joy for a mourning father Jacob as he remained sad for the rest of his life.

If Jacob knew that God had a plan and that his son Joseph would someday be found, his hope would have brought more of life to him at his old age when he reunited with his beloved son.

Unlike Jacob, God has not hidden his glorious plan from us. Recognizing the need to comfort His followers before His departure, Jesus said:

> *"Let not your heart be troubled; you believe in God, believe also in me. In my father's house are many mansions;*
>
> *if it were not so, I would have told you. I go to prepare a place for you.*
> *And if I go and prepare a place for you, I will come again and receive you; that where I am, there you may be also" (John 14:1-4).*

After completing His mission and He was departing the world, His disciples saw Him ascend into the sky. As they watched Him, they were sad. The only hope they had was leaving them in plain sight. Many of them had left their families and businesses to follow Jesus. The same Jesus was now leaving them.

How sad this must have been! Jesus recognized this situation, hence He sent two angels that appeared in form of men to comfort them. But notice what the two angels used to comfort the disciples. It was the promise of Jesus return and the final flight with Him:

> *"Now when He had spoken these things, while they watched, He was taken up, and a cloud received Him out of their sight.*

> *And while they looked steadfastly toward heaven as He went up, behold, two men stood by them in white apparel, who also said, "Men of Galilee", why do you stand gazing up into heaven?*

> *This same Jesus, who was taken up from you into heaven, will so come in like manner as you saw Him go into heaven" (Acts 1:9-11).*

The strongest way to give or receive comfort is to remember that Jesus is the God of all comforts as Paul says to the Corinthian church and our hope is renewed when we are reminded that this same Jesus will come back the same way to take away all who believe in Him forever

CHAPTER 13 – THE CONTROVERSY

About the time we were preparing to organize the Canada Walk 4 Jesus 2017, I approached many pastors and church leaders. In the process, I was exposed to the depth of disunity among the churches. I will speak more on the subject of unity in the next chapter.

But what is more concerning here is that the depth of disunity we are entangled in is somehow shifting our focus from a mindset for kingdom expansion and the readiness for the coming of the Lord and for the final flight.

We were organizing a video shoot describing this soon-to-happen event of the final flight in 2017. I approached a senior associate pastor of a major denomination in the city to invite him and his congregation to the event.

His response was much more staggering than the prior apathy to the subject of the final flight of the saints that I experienced with some other church leaders.

It is Controversial

The senior associate pastor said "we will not be participating or put poster on the wall for this event". I asked why and his reason was more daunting than his rejection: "we do not want our members to think we believe in this subject of the rapture. We have a lot of issues to deal with already. We don't want to start a new one".

So I asked him what he believed and if he believed in the subject. He reluctantly said it's not the kind of conversation he wanted to have at that moment. "I'm not a newsman. It's just you and I here. Do you believe in the final flight of the saints?" I pressed further. "hmn eh, I know Jesus will come someday." He yielded with careful affirmation.

This and several other instances have prompted me to try to address what I suspect are some of the controversies on the coming of Jesus and the final flight of His saints.

Jesus Comes Before the Antichrist

I saw a YouTube video with animations and it was indeed a movie. It was perfectly done on the subject of the final flight. I wanted to share the video as much as possible and promote it because of its message.

Unfortunately, I was unable to, because of a substantive error. The video claims that the Antichrist will be revealed and there will be Great Tribulation. It is then Jesus will come and take His believers away. This is wrong.

Although the spirit of the antichrist is currently fully at work, the antichrist will not be revealed to the world before Jesus comes, as some people have wrongly claimed.

Let's look at the scriptures that may have been misunderstood to inform this heresy. 1 Thessalonians 4, Paul said "by the word of the Lord", at the coming of Jesus, the dead in Christ shall rise first, those who are alive will be taken up with them to meet the Lord in the air.

In chapter 5 of the same scripture, see what the Holy Spirit told me has been a subject of misinterpretation. But praise God, He explains when we ask Him:

"But concerning the times and the seasons, brethren, you have no need that I should write to you.

For you yourselves know perfectly that the day of the Lord so comes as a thief in the night.
For when they say, "Peace and safety!" then sudden destruction comes upon them, as labor pains upon a pregnant woman.

And they shall not escape. But you, brethren, are not in darkness, so that this Day should overtake you as a thief.

You are all sons of light and sons of the day. We are neither of the night nor of darkness.

Therefore, let us not sleep, as others do, but let us watch and be sober.
For those who sleep, sleep at night, and those who get drunk are drunk at night But

let us who are of the day be sober, putting on the breastplate of faith and love, and as a helmet the hope of salvation.

For God did not appoint us to wrath, but to obtain salvation through our Lord Jesus Christ,

who died for us, that whether we wake or sleep, we should live together with Him." (1 Thessalonians 5:1-10)

It is important to understand the context of this scripture. Paul was responding to existing misunderstandings regarding the schedule for the end times. Hence, he says, "concerning the times and the seasons".

Second Coming –Day of the Lord
The Holy Spirit impressed on me that the Day of the Lord that Paul refers to here is the second coming of Jesus to the world to harvest the remnant of Israel and other believers who were left behind at His first return, but who will stay the course and not yield to the lordship of the antichrist by obtaining the mark of the beast.

Those saying peace and safety are those who have been deceived by the antichrist and have taken his seal of ownership. At His second coming, Jesus will be coming with the wrath of God to execute judgment on all the wicked, the Antichrist and Satan in what is known as the Battle of the Armageddon.

For those people who will suffer wrath with the enemy of God, "destruction will come upon them as labor pains upon a pregnant woman and they will not escape and this day will overtake them as a thief". This Day of the Lord is referenced severally by Old Testament prophets in the bible. It's the day God will execute judgment on the wicked.

Suddenly, a big black board appeared and suspended in the air right in my bonus room where I was. On the black board were many negative inscriptions

Those, like Paul, and you and I, who are of the day, will be sober, be vigilant and be ready to be taken away at Jesus' first return to the earth. Not in His second coming referred to in this scripture. We would have put on the breastplate of faith, love and helmet for the hope of salvation through the final flight with Jesus.

Whether or not we are on the earth or in paradise when the final flight with Jesus occurs, we would be with Jesus when He returns a second time to the earth and no doubts, will escape God's wrath that accompanies the second coming of Jesus. Instead, the bible indicates that we will fight alongside with Jesus in the victorious fight for the kingdom of God.

Yes, God did not appoint us unto wrath, but to obtain salvation through our Lord Jesus Christ. Certainly, the day of the Lord referenced in this scripture is not for the final flight. It is for the second coming of Jesus for battle. The same revelation is given by Jesus in Mathew 24 and unfortunately, is sometimes equally misunderstood.

Again, for the sake of clarity, there are two upcoming events describing the coming of Jesus to this world. They are the return of Jesus for the final flight of His saints, which is the focus of this book, and the second coming of Jesus.

In between these two is the reign of the Antichrist known as The Great Tribulation which will last for a total of seven years before Jesus' second coming. (Daniel 12:6, 7, 11, 12; Revelation 11:3, 12:14).

At His second coming, Jesus will bring along with Him His holy angels and all the believers that went to heaven with Him in the final flight.

His saints will have been empowered to face war but will not need to lift a sword. They will come to fight the Battle of the Armageddon against the antichrist, Satan and all the princes and demons.

This will be a simple victorious battle because of the supreme position of Jesus' power. But the destruction on the world and on all God's enemies will be so great. The scriptures below describe both the return of Jesus and the second coming of Jesus.

But unfortunately, they are often misconstrued to only be referencing the return of Jesus for the final flight, hence the erroneous doctrine that the antichrist will be revealed, and the believers will be in the world during The Great Tribulation:

> *"Now, brethren, concerning the coming of our Lord Jesus Christ and our gathering together to Him, we ask you, not to be soon shaken in mind or troubled,*

The above refers to the return of Jesus and the final flight of His saints, which is the focus of this book. Notice "concerning the coming of our Lord Jesus Christ and our gathering 'to' Him". Meaning our flight to meet Him in the air.

> *either by spirit or by word or by letter, as if from us, as though the day of Christ had come. Let no one deceive you by any means; for that Day will not come unless the falling away*

The day of Christ referenced here is not the same as the coming of the Lord Jesus" in the first part of this scripture. It refers to "the second coming of Jesus to the world". It is the day of vengeance and wrath of God upon all His enemies. It is the Great Day of the Lord referenced by several Old Testament prophets (Zephaniah 1:4, Isaiah 34:8, Joel 2:1).

The Thessalonian church were getting letters and rumors that supposedly were presented as though the letters had come from Paul the apostle. They feared that the day of the Lord had come perhaps because of the intensity of the persecution they faced from the Roman government, which was itself, some form of tribulation.

comes first, and the man of sin is revealed, the son of perdition, who opposes and exalts himself above all that is called God or that is worshiped, so that he sits as God in the temple of God, showing himself that he is God." (2 Thessalonians 2:1-4).

So Paul was breaking things down for them. He is saying here that the Day of vengeance, the second coming of Jesus or the Day of the wrath of the Lord will not come unless the falling away comes first (those who miss the final flight and are doomed) and the man of sin is revealed (the antichrist's reign, The Great Tribulation).

Both the return of Jesus for the final flight and the second coming of Jesus after the Great Tribulation are referenced in this scripture. *So,* Jesus will come first. The antichrist will follow, to commence the Great Tribulation and then the second coming of Jesus for the Battle of the Armageddon – the Great Day of the Lord.

Christians will not see Great Tribulation

In fact, to further the point that believers will not face the Great Tribulation, notice a pattern with the Passover in the scriptures. While the Egyptian slave masters were in deep mourning, the Israelites became wealthy and were rejoicing during their flight from Egypt.

I remember an open vision I received from Jesus couple of years ago. I was seated right on my couch after my quiet time in the morning. I was a little tired and sleepy, but I was awake. I felt someone tap me on the shoulder. At first, I thought it was my little one trying to get my attention.

As I opened my eyes, there was no one in the room. And I immediately knew it was the Lord. Then I said, speak Lord, your servant is listening. Suddenly, a big black board appeared and it was suspended in the air right in my bonus room where I was.

On the black board were many negative inscriptions in tiny fonts. Then on the top left corner of the blackboard is a big bold inscription written in upper cases. The Lord zoomed my eyes in to this bold inscription and it read: "WAR OF RECESSION".

The Holy Spirit impressed on me what this meant for the world in terms of global economic recession. Then I asked Him, what this means for Christians, His believers. His response was, "only the saved will be secure".

The black board disappeared. The open vision is God telling us that the world would experience a war of recession but the believers would be shielded from it. This vision was seen about 2 months before news stories ran in the media that there was another global recession under way and the stock market was crashing again.

The economic downturn happened and a lot of job losses resulted from it. But it was short. It is my belief that the open vision points beyond what happened. It points to what the world will experience before Jesus shows up in the sky.

What am saying here is that in this end time marking the coming of the Lord, there will be economic distress and scarcity of peace in the world, a problem to which the antichrist would first present himself as the solution after Jesus has come and gone with His believers.

But believers do not have to be broke to be ready for the return of Jesus. It is the intention of God to transfer the wealth of the wicked to the righteous people, in just the same way He did for Israel the night before they left Egypt.

There was a transfer of wealth as God caused the Egyptians to be favorable to Israel. They turned in their articles of gold and silver to Israel. Former Israeli slaves became wealthy overnight. The wealth was given to them because of God's plan ahead for them in the wilderness.

In the same way, believers should expect a transfer of wealth from the wicked to the righteous as the days draw nearer for the coming of Jesus.

This wealth transfer is not needed for our journey with Jesus. It is needed to demonstrate God's kindness towards His people even here on earth and to be used as resources for the last harvest of souls. Other activities that will usher in the return of Jesus are an increase in worship and praise to God as you will see later in this book.

Jesus Didn't Come Since Bible Days

Another common reason why there is some apathy, even among believers, towards the subject of the coming of Jesus and the final flight is the thought that early believers of Jesus in the bible thought Jesus would return in their lifetime but this never happened. So any attempt to say Jesus is coming soon to these believers is immediately dismissed.

They will say "soon" might be another 2,000 years. My take on this is that the early believers had this intense vertical focus on the coming of the Lord and the final flight because it is the Lord's desire for us in this church age to have the same mindset and focus.

The "it will soon happen" episode with the early believers in the bible was meant to serve as a template for how God expects us to live and be ready for Jesus' coming in our generation. The bible says that:

> *All Scripture is given by inspiration of God, and is profitable for doctrine, for reproof, for correction, for*

> *instruction in righteousness, that the man of*
> *God may be complete, thoroughly equipped*
> *for every good work (2 Timothy 3:16-17)*

So the scriptures indicating that early believers felt that the coming of Jesus would happen in their own days is given by inspiration of God for doctrine and instruction so we can use this as a template for living, be equipped for every good work, and of course, to be ready for the coming of Jesus.

Indeed, Jesus never intended to keep any of His believers in the dark about the day. That's why he gave numerous signs we should watch for that will point to the day. All the signs of the last days that Jesus describes for us, have been seen or accomplished.

For instance, He said the gospel of the kingdom will be preached to every nation. With the revolution in information technology especially social media, the gospel is being preached almost to every nation. So the next big event we should be waiting for now is the coming of Jesus and the final flight with Him.

Individual Prophecy

How do you pass the message that Jesus is coming back soon to someone who has received an individual prophecy that they will get married someday and that day is not soon? How do you convince someone that Jesus is coming very soon if they have been told they would become a pastor someday and that day is not soon?

How do you pass the same message to a mother who has received a prophecy that their five-year old son would someday become a medical doctor?

We are in the generation of prophecies, including false prophecies as the scriptures anticipated for the last days. The appetite for prophecies has increased. In Africa for example, many new people go with the title of the prophets and in many cases, there is a display of magic.

For those that have received individual prophecies genuinely from God, there is a number of things I would like for you to consider here.

First, Paul underscored the pivotal role of love among all virtues, gifts and fruits of the Holy Spirit (2 Corinthians 13:8). In the course of this, he lists prophecies as one of those things that will fail when pitted against love.

Second, would God continue to wait for His small P prophecies to be fulfilled on the earth which are increasing on a daily basis, before He chooses to fulfill His big P prophecies like the coming of Jesus?

Third, in the old testament of the bible, when God promised to come dwell among men, it must have been difficult for people of that generation to grasp how this kind of prophecy will be fulfilled. At the appropriate predestined time, God came in human flesh as Jesus Christ.

So the fulfillment of true prophecies in individual lives and the big P prophecies like the coming of Jesus all at the same time and within a very short unimaginable timeframe, is within the wisdom, omnipotence and omniscience nature of God.

Joshua completed a lessons learned report and evaluation study on God's faithfulness to His promises. I mean the Joshua in the bible. Not me. Here is the result of his finding: "Not a word failed of any good thing which the Lord had spoken to the house of Israel. All came to pass (Joshua 21:45).

Fourth, the nation of Israel didn't accept Jesus as the Messiah expected in prophecy. The reason for them expecting a different Messiah is because they had received a small P prophecy that the prophet Elijah would have to come back to the earth first before the real Messiah comes.

So that was partly the basis for their rejection of Jesus as many of them still expect a different Messiah. Unknown to them, according to Jesus' later revelation, Elijah had already come and gone. John the Baptist was the Elijah expected.

So it is possible that the small P prophecies that we hold on to as the basis for not seeing the imminence of the fulfillment of the big P policies may already have been fulfilled as God intends them without us knowing.

Fifth, Jesus never instructed that we should watch for prophecies to determine the day when He will return for the flight. He said we should watch for the signs (Mathew 24). And today, the signs of the end times are conclusively pervasive.

In addition to this, Jesus is giving revelation messages to several believers that He's coming very soon. So if anyone is so focused on the small P prophecies to the point they ignore to see the urgency of the big P prophecy written in the bible, they run the risk of suffering the same fate with the nation of Israel that missed out on a big P prophecy, the consequence many still suffer up till today.

The End Time Calendar

1. Jesus Returns for final flight	**2.** Christians leave the world	**3.** Antichrist rules the world
4. Christians at the banquet in heaven	**5.** The Great Tribulation in the world	**6.** Second Coming of Jesus
7. Battle of Armageddon	**8.** 1,000 Yrs. Millennial Reign of Christ	**9.** The Great White Throne Judgment
10. Death & Hell in Lake of Fire	**11.** A New Heaven & Earth	**12.** God dwells with mankind forever

Depart from me. I don't know you. You're a worker of iniquity. Who is He talking to?

CHAPTER 14- UNITY AND READINESS FOR THE FLIGHT

Jesus says *"Not everyone who says to Me, Lord, Lord, shall enter the Kingdom of heaven, but he who does the will of My Father in heaven. They will say to Me in that day, 'Lord, Lord, have we not prophesied in Your name, cast out demons, and done many wonders in Your name?'*

And I will declare to them, 'I never knew you; depart from Me, you who practice lawlessness! (Matthew 7:21-23)." I have often wondered to understand why these outcasts would have the confidence to argue their case even after judgment is set on their fate.

They most likely were believers who may have been cumulatively disobedient. Disobedience or rebellion to God is like the sin of witchcraft (1 Samuel 15:23). They may have been committing sin but thought that since the healing anointing was still flowing, that's an indication that God approved of them.

They may have compromised the savior Jesus, and have gotten power to perform miracles from the devil. Whatever the case may be, they will have gained the whole world and lost their own souls in the process. Let's work our salvation with fear and trembling, as the scripture instructs.

Healing Anointing not Enough

Let me alert you to something in the bible. The prophet Elisha died and was buried in the tomb. Some Israelites were going to bury a dead man before they spotted a band of raiders on their way. They quickly threw the dead body into Elisha's tomb. The bible says that when the dead body came in contact with Elisha's bones, the man came to life (2 Kings 13:21).

I believe God is using this scripture to demonstrate what He would later say in the New Testament that the gifts and the calling of God are irrevocable (Romans 11:29). Even in death, Elisha raised the dead. A person can be spiritually dead and still be flowing in the healing anointing.

Avoid Persistent Disobedience

Avoid persistent disobedience. Sometimes we as believers may miss things when it comes to obeying God and His instructions, especially as a result of fear. Doing this persistently or encouraging this in others by the system we put in place will amount to rebellion towards God.

I remember some time ago, a sister was describing to me how God gave her instructions to go and address a specific situation. As soon as she began speaking, the Holy Spirit said to me to notice the error in what she was about to say.

She had been woken up in the middle of the night and was instructed to write down the instruction. She was asked to go to a specific sister in a different local church which was part of her parent church.

The Holy Spirit gave her the name, picture description and the exact church address where this other sister worshiped. She was told to tell this sister that she should not make the decision she was about to make regarding her marriage. And in obedience, off she went the next morning looking for the exact district church.

She located the church and met with the pastors. She gave a vivid description of the sister in question with her name. They confirmed the description as one of their members. She then gave the message to the pastors for them to relay it to the sister in question. And she left.

So I asked if she went back to confirm that they gave the message to the sister in question. She said "oh no. I have done my part. It's up to them. They have authority over their congregation." And this is true.

We must respect authority. Pastors have authority over the congregation and so is government over the citizens. We must pray for authority. Sometimes, when an instituted authority is rebellious, God may allow for an override of such authority to bring sanity.

And if you are used in this sanity process, you have to be careful. God does not condone that as a habit for His children. The reason is because Satan did that to God. However, in the case of this sister, she had not fully obeyed God. No, that's not accurate. She had not obeyed God at all. Obedience is doing what God instructs and intends, the time He intends it to be done, the way He wants it done, by whom He wants it done and for whom He wants it done.

King Saul in the bible has always been used as the classic example of lessons of disobedience. But when I looked closely with empathy, at his situation and the circumstances surrounding his disobedience, I concluded that I myself and any God-fearing person would have done the same thing Saul did if we were in his shoes.

But nonetheless, this simple mistake amounted to disobedience to God's command even though it was not Saul's intention to disobey God. It cost Saul the kingdom of Israel (1 Samuel 13:5-15). Moses could not enter the promise land with his people Israel because he did not fully obey God's instruction.

However, thank God. We are not under law, but under the grace of Jesus. Our simple, innocent mistake will not attract God's judgment. Bless God for Jesus. But we must understand that Saul's and Moses' stories underscore how seriously God sees disobedience to the point He compares it to the sin of witchcraft.

With the New Testament grace that Jesus brings, for disobedience resulting from fear or ignorance, God's mercy is available to forgive. But it is difficult to not think we are abusing the grace when the fear and ignorance factors are removed and our persistent disobedience results from the decision to want to satisfy ourselves as opposed to God's commands.

Cumulatively, this may put us in the same category as the five foolish virgins at the final flight. It may put us in the same category with those that will be given the verdict: "depart from me".

I think the sister's response was a result of wrong indoctrination that any message from God to the congregation must come from the spiritual leaders or pastors. In the process, she disobeyed the Holy Spirit. She was instructed to deliver a critical message to a specified person.

But out of respect for a human authority, she gave the message to someone else. You ask yourself, couldn't the Holy Spirit have given the message directly to the pastor or the elders in the local church of the sister to whom God was sending instruction regarding her marriage?

Perhaps they were already in the know. Perhaps, the Holy Spirit didn't want them to know. Perhaps He felt the pastor was too loaded with tasks and he had his hands full already. In His wisdom, the Holy Spirit gave the message to a complete stranger to achieve certain effects in the situation.

But human notion of spiritual authority stood in way of the Holy Spirit. I do not see any blame in this sister and I believe that the Holy Spirit that alerted me to a sincere error in her judgment feels exactly the same way about her. Up until the time I pointed this to her, she had not realized she had made a mistake.

She ended the explanation of how she carried out the instruction feeling satisfied. She is a daughter of the Most High and she still remains steadfast in her service to God. But she had been a victim of an overblown human tradition in kingdom work that places too much emphasis on submission to a human spiritual authority than obedience to God.

I too have been in her shoes in the past. In a church where I served, the night before, I was woken up about three times before daybreak. I had made a decision that I would not get on the pulpit to minister the next day which was a Sunday. And the Lord knew exactly why. But He wanted me to get on it to address a specific situation. Even after giving me the same instruction for about three times, I was still reluctant.

I didn't want to be seen like I was doing what I had not been authorized by human beings to do. But I eventually yielded in obedience and stood on the pulpit to deliver the message.

After the service, a brother approached me and thanked me for my obedience in coming up to speak saying he was the one that was about to make a decision regarding his situation which the Lord was warning against. I told him he was not the one. It was a different family the Lord had shown me.

As it turned out, there were several cases of the same issue in the same local church which the Lord wanted to address. But the circumstances then and human notion of spiritual authority almost stood in the way of my obedience.

In another instance, Jesus showed me two different people in a vision that I didn't know, who had a stroke condition. One of them was a woman who said to me how painful it was to watch someone steal her money and unable to do something about it because at that point, she was having a stroke attack.

One day in a church. I was asked to lead prayers and it was impressed on me that that woman was in church while I was leading the prayers. Just before I was about to think about how to ask who it was and invite her to pray for her, the pastor pressed forward as if to tell me to hand over the microphone.

My knowledge of that environment didn't allow me to think and perhaps tell the pastor about what had just been impressed on me that the Lord wants to heal someone. I quickly handed the microphone to the pastor and jolted to my seat.

It was all my fault. I repented from this and I still feel sorry for the lady with a stroke condition each time I remember her story. The point of this is that we need to allow for a system within our local churches that doesn't stifle obedience to the higher spiritual authority – the God – head.

What is more concerning here is that those people Jesus will tell to depart from Him seem to believe that they qualify for the flight.

Remember the parable of the ten virgins that Jesus narrated in the bible (Matthew 25:1-13). They were all virgins expecting the bridegroom. Each of them had a lamp with oil to keep it burning. Unfortunately, five of them didn't have enough oil to keep their lamp burning.

When the groom came, it was too late to look for oil. They were shut out from the wedding ceremony. They were born again because they had a lamp. They were baptized in the Holy Spirit because they had oil. But they were still not ready. I pray for you and myself that this will not be our fate in Jesus name. Amen!

Keep the Unity and the Bond of the Spirit
As individual believers of Jesus, one way to be prepared and be ready for the coming of Jesus and the final fight with Him is to ensure we are not in disunity with His spiritual body. I say spiritual body because not all churches are of Christ and not all who profess to know Jesus actually truly are His.

Disunity doesn't happen just because there are differences in denominations, doctrines and churches. Often times Jesus is glorified in the differences. Unity of the body of Christ is not a call to integrate denominations. Unity is prelude to revival in any case.

But a refusal to agree to unite behind a mutual kingdom purpose for Jesus, is evidence of the devil at work. The reason for this is that the refusal is often premised on "my church", "my members", "I don't want to be seen with those as they are not Christians", "he took my members away" "they left my church" etc.

In all these, you see evidence of a mission accomplished by those who have received marching orders from the Hades as I describe it through an open vision later in this book.

Those who have received marching orders for disunity include a competition spirit, a familiar (impersonation) spirit, a religious spirit and a territorial spirit. That's why when you leave a work place, a send-off party is organized by those who have not seen the light. But sometimes when you leave a church that may be the end of your relationship with the pastor or the members.

The four spirits I listed above are responsible for it. I pray that the Spirit of God will awaken our churches to recognize this spiritual problem and work together to come out of it.

There is no perfect church. When there is an issue in a church, as a child of God, you help to resolve it if it's within your capacity to do so.

Pray for your pastors and leaders because as the bible says, the enemy always likes to strike the Sheppard so that the sheep will scatter. He did it to Jesus and all His disciples flee away.

He is doing it today to spiritual leaders and without your prayers; the enemy will have his way. Notice something at the garden of Gethsemane when Jesus requested prayers from His followers. Jesus knew He would soon be stricken by the crucifiers and be taken to the Cross. It was the climax of His mission on earth and He was ready for it.

But He was sad and wept bitterly in His human form knowing that when He goes to hell on our behalf, He would be separated from the trinity for the first time in eternity past, eternity present and eternity future.

So He repeatedly requested His inner circle friends, Peter, James and John to pray for Him as He Himself prays to the Father in Heaven (Luke 22:39-45).

In the same way, many spiritual leaders in the church are facing a similar Gethsemane situation in different scales. Pray for them, encourage them. When you see things that are not right and a pastor or a spiritual leader seems to be abusing their power and position, prayerfully take the matter to God and approach them with the aim of redeeming the church and the leaders concerned.

As a child of God that is getting ready for the final flight with Jesus, don't join others in spreading gossip. If you hear something not right about a leader, approach them directly with the mindset of redeeming the situation to glorify God. Don't be dismissive of what you hear either, as this might be the only chance a believer who is backsliding might be saved from falling.

When a believer is not fleeing from every appearance of evil, they may be in danger of backsliding. When a believer has sinned, they should seek forgiveness and repent immediately. When a believer is sinning without repenting, they are backslidden. This is the time we pray for them and should go after them with the hope they will be restored to faith.

But when a once spirit-filled believer now publicly speaks against the belief in the Holy Spirit, Jesus and God, they are fallen from grace to grass and there is no getting back up (Hebrews 6:4). Consider the stakes that are high. A fallen believer will suffer greater punishment in the hands of Satan in hell. The reason for this is that Satan will be more upset with them because they have helped contribute to God's kingdom while on earth.

The bible says judgment will begin at the house of God. Consider the loss of the kingdom of God and let this judge your action in situations like this. Don't be jumping from church to church but spend time to pray for your local church and pastors.

By the grace of God, I have stood side by side with fellow believers in trials to the point I survived being strangled, being threatened multiple times with guns in my sleep, with a warning "don't go to that church!" But God stood by me because of His loving kindness.

I have also on many occasions gone for a church service simply because I wanted to keep the minister encouraged to keep pursuing what God has called them to do. After feeling like I wanted to leave a church, I have deliberately tried to wait to leave it in good shape before I left.

This again is the mind of Christ for us as God's children. Here or there, it is the same Body of Christ. It is godly living! It is God's desire for us to have a kingdom mindset in these end times

However, if you are noticing a pattern of lying and manipulations in a pastor or spiritual leader, you have the authority to respectfully approach them on this issue before things fall apart. It doesn't matter how big their works of miracle or prophecy may be. They may even play the "spiritual authority" card with you.

If not careful, you yourself will be a victim of their manipulations. I remember the Holy Spirit saying to me some time ago, "Look unto Jesus, the Apostle and the High Priest of your faith" (Hebrews 3:3). If you confirm this pattern and they refuse to change, you are authorized by God to run as fast as possible from the church.

You are not by any means bound to any church. You belong to the spiritual body of Christ and all His body parts are represented physically in different churches. But remember to continue praying for the church, the members and pastors even after you have left.

You should never be satisfied that others risk losing the final flight with Jesus and the heavenly kingdom. This is godly living! If God asks you to leave your church because He has an assignment for you, you have to obey God notwithstanding the situation.

And if for any other reason you feel the need to leave, approach the pastor or the spiritual leader when your decision has been made.

Request from them how they intend for you to leave and work with them for your exit. Don't leave with a fight. And when you leave, don't take others with you. Be careful to leave the bond of the spirit intact.

Even after taking all the right steps at your exit, unfortunately it doesn't mean things will go well. You only have control over your own action, not over the actions of others.

But in doing this, you will show that you are the true child of your heavenly father. Remember, the scripture says, "if it is possible, as much as depends on you, live peaceably with all men" (Romans 12:18). Some situations don't depend on you

Don't join others in breaking a church apart. Sometimes there may have been situations that warranted it especially when the devil has taken over at the center. But be sure to reconcile with well-meaning true believers in the process, as much as it depends on you.

As a spiritual leader or pastor, never be disgruntled or become so offended that a member or leader leaves your church. And don't make enemies of the ones that leave or of those to whom they go. At the exit of a believer from a local church, if things are not handled properly, we may invite the power of darkness to take advantage of the situation.

Satan's familiar spirits (impersonating spirits) are deployed especially if a fight or disgruntleness is involved. The exiting believer is entangled in unnecessary spiritual warfare, delaying their recovery and preparation for whatever kingdom purpose God has for them.

They also see you in the middle of this warfare as an adversary since you are impersonated and presented to them as the adversary. The vibrations of this will sometimes impact your own gathering.

> *Destiny of Israel delayed for extra 30 years because Moses was not ready*

Prerogative Purpose

Let me share with you a word I received from Jesus in March 2016. I was going to preach a message that God gave me for a particular church. The message was titled "The Power of Humility" and of course, Moses was one of several examples I was going to talk about based on several things the Lord told me about him.

I recall that when I wrote down the message, I was just about to exit my office den used as a prayer room, when the Holy Spirit restrained me from proceeding further out of the room. He asked me to write down the message He had given me and instructed me on what to write.

The next day, He asked me to add something about Rebecca to it. So, on the day I was to deliver the message to that church, I drove to the premises and just before entering it, the Jesus spoke to me again.

And here is what He said: "Joshua". I said "yes Lord". Then He proceeds:

> *"Do you know that the destiny of Israel was delayed in Egypt for another 30 years because Moses was not ready?"*

The above is an example of the manifestation of the word of wisdom that Paul lists in his description of the different manifestations of the Holy Spirit in 1 Corinthians 12.

Word of wisdom is manifested when there is a revealed knowledge of the kingdom that is not in the bible but that seeks to explain what is in the bible.

The knowledge comes directly from the Holy Spirit because he authored the bible by inspiring righteous men to put it in ink. Israel was prophesied and expected to be enslaved in Egypt for 400 years. But they left Egypt 30 years more than expected.

The Holy Spirit told me that the reason for this was because Moses was going through a preparation process that included coming to a point he would be so humble that he would not trust in himself in anyway. And because Moses had not got to this state, he was not ready for the purpose ahead.

As I drove into the church, I was stunned by the word I had just received. I began to ponder on this. So, as long as Moses was not ready, Israel would remain in captivity in Egypt.

In spite of their cries from excruciating suffering in Egypt, the people of God would remain in the condition as long as the man God has destined to effect their deliverance was not ready for the mission.

So, God would not send someone else. It had been firmly decided in the mind of God that when it comes to the deliverance of Israel, it had to be Moses.

I then realized why when Moses offered Aaron his brother as an alternative to him for the mission, God told Moses He would make him like a god and Aaron his prophet.

Later, when Moses was still hesitant for the mission, God wanted to kill him, but thanks to his wife Zipporah who appealed to God by smearing blood on Moses' leg. This kind of a unique and specific divine purpose that cannot be transferred to another person is what I call prerogative purpose.

There are other examples of this in the bible. Abraham and Sarah's healing from barrenness falls within the prerogative purpose of God. Zechariah and Elizabeth's healing from barrenness also falls within this prerogative purpose. Consider Simeon.

Simeon had been told by the Holy Spirit that he would not see death until his eyes has seen the Messiah Jesus. It was his destiny to fulfill that purpose. No one else, even though Anna the prophetess was given a similar purpose.

No one would replace Simeon's role and he was not allowed to die until Jesus came. He must have been very old and eager to depart to paradise.

But God would not transfer Simeon's unique and purposeful assignment to someone else. It is a prerogative purpose and there is no escape for Simeon from it. Jonah was another example of a prerogative purpose carrier. God sent him to go to Nineveh and warn the city to repent from sin and turn to God otherwise God would execute His judgment on them. Jonah cowardly bowed out of the errand. He was afraid of being labelled a false prophet because he knew that God would forgive Nineveh after they repent.

Absconding to Tarshish, the ship he traveled on was bombarded by a devastating storm to the point his co-passengers and mariners realized that the storm has a supernatural cause. They cast a lot to know who on board the ship has made their god angry and the lot fell on Jonah.

The storm did not stop bombarding the ship until Jonah was thrown overboard and was swallowed up by the big fish inside which he eventually repented and obeyed God to go to Nineveh (Jonah 1).

The point here is that Jonah had a prerogative purpose. God could have sent someone else since He has many prophets. But when it comes to Nineveh's repentance, it had to be Jonah. No one else. Now pay attention to this. The bible did not say that God sent the storm to Jonah and his co-passengers. Remember, the bible says disobedience is like the sin of witchcraft.

It is possible that the supernatural storm came from the other side of darkness – from Satan himself. The evil ones know when we are disobedient to God and they capitalize on that. And since we are holding on to the sin of disobedience which is a mark of witchcraft, we may attract storms.

I am bringing this topic up because there may be some Moseses in our churches with a prerogative purpose.

We should be careful to not stand in the way of their obedience or delay it. There are people waiting on the other end of that obedience. There may be people on wheelchair, whose healing or breakthrough falls within the prerogative purpose of God.

As Israel's enslavement and deliverance were matters bigger than Israel, so is the healing and breakthrough for those waiting on the other end of obedience of prerogative purpose carriers. That's why you will see people needing healing and deliverance and have done everything necessary to obtain it.

They have the faith, they approach reputable healing and deliverance ministers and they even witness others getting their own healing. Their condition may fall within the prerogative purpose of God. It's got nothing to do with them and no wrong may have come from them. They are a blessing in disguise to the point that their situation fits within the prerogative purpose of God. And their healing or deliverance is intricately linked to a particular, specific deliverer: a Moses, an Abraham, a Zechariah, a Jonah and a Simeon.

The sooner we enable and release or enable them within our congregations, for their prerogative purpose, the better the Kingdom of God for it. Notice what God said when Moses was eventually ready for the mission: "And the LORD said: "I have surely seen the oppression of My people who *are* in Egypt, and have heard their cry because of their taskmasters, for I know their sorrows" (Exodus 3:7).

So God had surely heard their cry, seen their oppression long before He spoke to Moses about it. But He would not do anything on this earlier because the one He had chosen to use for their deliverance was not ready. This leads me to another important subject, which is spiritual leadership.

Spiritual Leadership

We need to be sensitive to the Holy Spirit and not limit His power to choose whoever He wants to serve as leaders or fulfill certain tasks in His spiritual church. Sometimes we condition Him to use whoever we put in position based on our own sentiments without asking Him to choose who He really wants.

He is gentle and He has a mission to fulfill and so He would sometimes do what we ask Him, but with very limited use, hence kingdom advancement is stifled and sometimes His prerogative purpose is delayed because the corresponding purpose carrier is not given a chance.

We should remember we will someday stand before Jesus and give account of our actions. Nepotism has eaten deep into Christian worship. I hear of cases in Europe, America and Africa where highly massive churches are handed over to young people who were never ordained by God but they make the cut because their parents founded the church.

Qualified, founding members of the church are pushed aside, resulting into disunity. Jesus said, upon this rock "I will build my church and the gates of hell shall not prevail against it".

Look at the personal pronoun, "I" and the possessive pronoun, "my". With this He indicates that not only does He own His church, but that He retains the right to do whatever He pleases with it.

We are custodians of His church. In line with what Jesus says in this scripture, and in this building project, we are not the owners, we are not His co-builders, nor are we his foremen. We don't even make the cut to be the chief corner stone, because Jesus is. The closest position we occupy in the building project is the building blocks which He molds.

Don't get me wrong. There are instances where the father is called as a priest and the child is, as well. In fact, this is the ideal situation. Priests should begat priests. But sometimes destinies are different. And when they are the same in the priestly line, unless we have asked God and God confirms our child should replace us in succession, we may risk refusing Jesus the right which He stresses that it is His own in the scripture above. They may be in the priestly line but our altar might not be the right soil for them.

God might have even a bigger or perhaps, a prerogative purpose for them to fulfill elsewhere. By keeping them in the wrong soil to protect our own interest, we may be delaying their obedience, hence denying those who are waiting to receive the benefits of it on the other end. We are also mortgaging what God wants to accomplish through others in the wrong soil we put them.

I remember some time ago a young man was to do some work for me. He had been introduced to me by a friend. And over the week, Jesus showed me in a twin vision this young man on the stage preaching powerfully.

When I ran into Him on the train, I asked him, "has God been telling you things?" He said no. I asked again, "are you born again?" He said yes.

Then I told Him what God had been telling me about him that he was supposed to be a preacher. The young man burst out laughing – "hahaha. My father is a Reverend in Africa. He has always tried to get me to become a pastor in his church." "Why have you been refusing", I asked. His answer is saddening – "I want to be young and rich." Of course I counseled him.

But three things we can learn from this man's example. The first is that yes, God sometimes calls the child to a ministerial priesthood as He called the parents. Second is that there is a possibility the priestly father had given the wrong impression to the young man that serving God equates to being poor.

The third is that the father's approach may be wrong. He may not have allowed the child to identify his destiny that God was calling him into kingdom service. Instead, he may have watered down his interest by calling him to serve the interest of his father to take over a priestly business that, to this young man, was not lucrative.

Whatever the case may be, what am saying here is that we need to be careful in selecting leaders. How did Jesus select spiritual leaders? Notice these two examples we can learn from. When Jesus was told that His earthly mother and brothers had arrived, He dismissed them:

"But He answered and said to the one who told Him, "Who is My mother and who are My brothers?" And He stretched out His hand toward His disciples and said, "Here are My mother and My brothers! For whoever does the will of My Father in heaven is My brother and sister and mother."(Mathew 12:47-50).

This is one indication that Jesus did not allow nepotism to creep into the Father's business. Secondly, Jesus did not allow His emotional sentiment to cloud His judgment in selecting a leader for his church.

Jesus had a favorite among His twelve disciples. His name is John. He is called John the Beloved because Jesus has a special place in His heart for this disciple.

At one point when all twelve were gathered with Jesus, it was John who reclined in the table with Jesus. However, note that Jesus does not discriminate. There are unique attributes in the life of this disciple that earned him a special place in the heart of the Lord.

But notice what happened when Jesus was to appoint a leader for His church. He chose Peter not just because Peter showed leadership aptitude. He chose Peter as the head of the church because the Father in heaven had revealed to Peter that Jesus was the Son of God.

This was an indication to Jesus that a leader had been chosen out of the twelve from heaven. Even though He has authority over His ministry, and He has a favourite among the twelve, Jesus still felt that the Father's kingdom business transcends His personal feelings. We will be better served and the kingdom better served as well if we follow the example of Jesus in selecting spiritual leaders.

Send Them Off Like Moses' Mother

Here is God's way of sending people off for their kingdom purpose from the church. Do what the Moses' mother did (Exodus 2). She saw that the baby Moses was beautiful. She did not want to let him go as she is emotionally attached to him. She feels she needs to protect him from the murderous pharaoh. But she realized Moses was beautiful with a purpose.

Keeping him in hiding for longer might endanger her life and that of the baby. She took a bold step, made an ark for the baby and placed him by the river banks with the hope that Pharaoh's daughter may pick him up to raise him. She supplied the immediate need of the baby.

She asked Moses' sister to watch over him from afar. When a member of our church has a kingdom purpose, we may be too attached to them. But we have to let go. And letting go means we support them for the kingdom purpose. It means we continue watching out for them in prayers as the baby's sister was asked to do.

He Will Not Always Speak to Us

When it comes to His corporate establishments like His church, Jesus will not always speak to us, even though we are the leader He has put in place. We need to realize that at the moment we appoint members of the board of directors or workers, since it's Jesus' establishment, He has accepted them as channels of instructions as well. When Solomon was to start building the temple, God anointed his men with wisdom and all the skills needed to execute the building project (Exodus 31).

In the same way, God anoints the workers in the church. He may choose to speak through them regarding the building of the church. Like Solomon, the leader receives the vision for the temple. He translates it into a mission for the builders. And God provides the wisdom on how the building work proceeds through the foremen in the building project.

We need to humbly accept this blessing from God for the church to realize its full potential in Christ Jesus. Peter was the senior pastor of the New Testament church in the bible. When the Holy Spirit has a word for his congregation, the bible did not say it was released through Peter (Acts 32:12).

When the apostles in Jerusalem heard that the people of Samaria had received Jesus, the bible says, they sent Peter and John to Samaria (Acts 8:14), to follow up. Wasn't Peter the supreme leader among them? They sent him with prayers, indicating he had some people he was accountable to even though he was the leader.

Finally, Peter must have been quite humble to accept a public rebuke from Paul when Peter tried to be politically correct in not publicly associating with the gentiles. I remember the planning for the Canada Walk 4 Jesus event. My mind was completely loaded with planning to the point

I knew that God was trying to speak to me but it wasn't filtering through my spirit. Thankfully, I had been so open-minded with the team to feel free to let me know if they receive any word concerning the event.

And yes, God gave direction through one of them and this changed the trajectory of our planning. As we prepare for the return of Jesus, we need to pay attention to internal issues within the church so we are not sidetracked from a needed attention to the last harvest of souls.

Avoid Pulpit Fight

We sometimes invite someone who had given up on the idea of going to church because of incessant conflict, quarrels and in-fighting. Nothing can be more frustrating than to see that person trying out church again after a long time and the preacher can be easily noticed expressing they have personal issues with some folks in the congregation. This happens.

I hope we don't discourage a new comer or a new convert from coming to church by our actions. If there are internal rancour in the leadership, let's deal with it off the pulpit. The congregations need not see conflict. They are tired from the conflicts in the world. They have come to a place of refuge from them.

> *We are all running the same race,*
> *though we may be on different tracks.*

Avoid Competition

Avoid being entangled in competition with other Christians or ministers. Our competition is against the kingdom of darkness to win territories for the Lord. Not with ourselves.

There is the devil's competition spirit. Don't get trapped by it. Avoid the quest for fame and wealth. Pursue the kingdom purpose and pursue it with others. We are all running the same race, though we may be on different tracks.

Everyone who makes it to the finish line gets a prize. Yes, it is hard. One way I make sure I am free from this kind of entanglement is to support others in whatever God has called them to do, with my resources, time, prayers and ideas.

Reward Not By Numbers

In God's end time calendar that I describe even with a chart in previous pages, there is the Great White Throne Judgment. It is the judgment of reward for service to God while on earth. But here's what we need to know: God's reward system is not based on human wisdom of numerical proportionality. Jesus once indicated that the first shall be the last and vice versa.

I remember having some conversation with a minister some time ago on the reward for the servants of God. He mentioned big names in ministry and had this impression that their rewards for service in heaven will be based on how many souls they have won into the kingdom.

I asked him, "what about those who have been called to be worship leaders?" they may have led only a few people to the Lord in their lifetime but were obedient in serving the Lord as they were called to. I put this to you, what about Stephen in the bible, the first martyr of Jesus?

Stephen never led a single soul to the Lord but he was stoned to death while preaching. The bible says that *"while the earth remains, seedtime and harvest, cold and heat, winter and summer, and day and night shall not cease"* (Genesis 8:22). This Noahic covenant that God made has stood the test of time in spite of the climate change or global warming.

It says as long as the earth exists, seed time and harvest time shall not cease. This covenant applies to everything on the face of the earth, including soul-winning. When it comes to soul-winning, there are seeders and harvesters. Who gets to be the harvester depends on whether the soul is ready for harvest.

When you see a sinner raise their hands up in church in surrender to the Lord as the preacher makes invitation, there are seeders that have contributed to that decision.

They may have contributed in prayers, in speaking to the sinner in the past or in even repeatedly inviting them to church. There are worshipers who usher in the presence of the Holy Spirit who does the actual conversion.

When you see a sinner raise their hands up in church in surrender to the Lord as the preacher makes invitation, there are seeders that have contributed to that decision

So we are all laborers in God's kingdom service. The extent to which we obey the Lord will determine the extent of the reward we get, in addition to the Lord's own wisdom in applying rewards as He knows our hearts. And spending our time to support others in what God has called them to do even when it impacts the time needed to pursue our own is a time well spent and will be richly rewarded. King David fought many victorious battles. But guess what? The mighty men that fought with him were not forgotten. They were remembered by God. They were rewarded with their names engraved in what I call God's Hall of Fame.

With remarkable detail, God remembers the acts of valor by each of David's men one by one, on this Hall of Fame (2 Samuel 23:8-31). Be a smart investor. Sow into the ministerial businesses of others. You will be storing up for yourself greater treasures in heaven.

In fact, though the thought of the reward for the faithful servant should give us incentive to serve and obey, our motivation for obedience should be because we love Jesus. So there is no basis for competition.

Rugged Integrity

On the subject of integrity, I am not referring to stealing from the offering bag or siphoning money from the church for personal gains. I am not talking about refusing to acknowledge our colleagues at work that they have done well. I am not talking about cheating others or lying about others, knowing that the position we occupy commands trust to the point that we are believed and those we lie about are at the receiving end.

We know that those who do these things are definitely not waiting for Jesus and the final flight with Him. What am talking about here is rugged integrity. Integrity of heart that commands God's attention. When Nathaniel was told that Jesus has been discovered, he said about the Jesus he has not yet met, "can any good thing come out of Nazareth?"

This same unpolished, politically incorrect disciple still commanded attention from Jesus because of the integrity of his heart. Jesus says of Nathaniel: "[...] Behold, an Israelite indeed, in whom is no deceit!"(John 1:47).

After the generous giving by him and his people towards the building of the temple of the Lord, king David indicates God's emphasis on the state of the heart when giving as something much more valuable than the outward appearance of the gifts and offerings to God themselves:

> *"O LORD our God, all this abundance that we have prepared to build You a house for Your holy name is from Your hand, and is all Your own.*
>
> *I know also, my God, that You test the heart and have pleasure in uprightness. As for me, in the uprightness of my heart I have willingly offered all these things;*
>
> *and now with joy I have seen Your people, who are present here to offer willingly to You. O LORD God of Abraham, Isaac, and Israel, our fathers, keep this forever in the intent of the thoughts of the heart of Your people, and fix their heart toward You.(1 Chronicles 29:16-18)*

That is rugged integrity! It is the integrity that focuses every action we take on the state of the heart when we take it. David was able to defend this before God for himself and his people because his focus has always been how God will see the state of his heart when making sacrifice to him.

In giving, service to God and people, God values the humble, pure, truthful, generous, and sincere motives from our heart and spirit. These motives will be a huge part of our reward for service here on earth and for eternity, will be computed.

You Belong to the Praying Team

Prayers in the New Testament church are not intended to be patterned along the Old Testament ways. Yes, there is the ministry of intercession similar to the watch men in Isaiah 62. But every believer of Christ has been called to the praying team, without exception. The New Testament church cannot realize its full potential if we continue to go with the practice where only a few join the praying team.

Jesus said, watch and pray so that you don't fall into temptation (Matthew 26:41). He was saying that prayer is a guard against the risk of falling into sin, which may disqualify us for the final flight. The bible also says we should pray without ceasing (1 Thessalonians 5:17). This is not a figurative expression. It is not an hyperbole. It is to be taken literally.

Pray, 24 hours a day, 7 days a week, and 365 days a year. It is God setting His expectation for the time desired for communication and worship to Him by His children. Humanly speaking, we are unable to meet this target because of legitimate things that pertain to life and Godliness, including the spread of the gospel.

But God expects us to aspire towards this target by increasing the time spent with Him. The reason is because He is preparing us for the glorious flight and the destination where it will be all about worship and prayers only, to Him.

Jesus echoed the Old Testament belief that "My house shall be a house of prayers". It's interesting how much little time we devote to prayers in our churches. Even the mid-week prayer meeting is attended by only a handful of people. Corporate prayers are very essential. As the bible says, one can only chase a thousand. Two has a multiplying effect to chase ten thousand.

When you see the few people attending corporate prayers, they are usually healthier believers than the rest of the congregation. The next time your pastor calls for prayers, be the first to be there. Be the one praying for people and not the one being prayed for.

Sometimes am in a busy place with no opportunity to pray. I just grab my phone, put it to my ear and start praying to God, speaking to Him even in public. People around think am talking to someone on the phone.

Well, they may be right. But in this case, it is a special someone. Without observing any secret service protocol, I have a direct call to the King of kings, the President and Commander in Chief of the combined terrestrial and celestial military force. Praise be to the Lord Jesus for this direct access.

On Racial Division and Diversity

While the African church is carried away by inordinate affection for wealth and corruption, the American church has been negatively divided along racial lines for decades. The division mirrors the division in the nation itself. Racism should not be tolerated in the Body of Christ.

Jesus prayed in John 17 that all His believers will be in unity so that the world may believe. Which means unity is prelude to revival. Here is what drew my attention to this issue.

In 2017, the national convention of a major church denomination in the United States initially refused to pass a resolution to condemn White Supremacy and all forms of their racist and hateful ideologies at a point when their fellow Christians of color were on the edge for their lives as racism and hatred was emboldened.

The convention eventually passed the resolution after their refusal went viral on social media and in the public.

But this revealed a deeper than imagined racial division within the US church. While I was concerned for this, Jesus told me that Canada church is not immune to the issue.

The division has been worsened in recent times. We hear reports of people leaving the church in the United States because pastors have turned the pulpit to partisan political platforms. The church is increasingly divided between democrats and republicans – in my view, modern variants of their biblical counterparts- Pharisees and Sadducees.

Jesus was not a fan of either of them. Yes I may register with any of them to fulfill my civic responsibility and in voting for those I believe will serve the interest of God and the people. But I refuse to be identified as a conservative or a liberal.

The heavenly Kingdom of God that John describes in the book of revelation is very diverse with all nations on earth praising God. So will be the journey to it

Neither of these two appellations fully conveys the identity of Christ to which I am obligated to ascribe to, given our imperfections. So I am not a liberal Christian. Neither am I a conservative Christian. I am a Jesus Christian.

And that's the viewpoint I believe Christians should have. Our righteous and justified disagreement with the other side should never be allowed to be reduced to a battle of "us versus them".

We have been tasked by Jesus to bring the message of the kingdom to all and win them over to the Light. Therefore, we should never give any impressions that we are their enemies. That's what the devil wants.

There is nothing wrong in a Christian throwing their weight behind a policy objective that serves the interest of our faith in line with the bible. This means, support for the republican that wants to slow down the killing of unborn children through abortion and support for the democrat who wants to do the same for the children that are out of the womb through common sense gun regulations.

And ultimately, it means support for especially believers who are impacted by the evils of racism and hatred. Support for the course against bullying and violence of all forms to all people.

Christians should not be mislabeled as haters. Without Christians in this world, evil would have multiplied exponentially. We are the light of the world. Without us, the world will be buried in deep darkness.

And this is not a word of condemnation on anyone. This is a call for true believers, especially those in position of influence in the church, to guard their identity in Christ, be consistent in standing for truth, and take deliberate actions in dealing with these issues.

In the book of Acts chapter 6, the bible indicates that a complaint on racial discrimination among the disciples of Jesus came in against the Hebrews by the Hellenists (Greeks), because their widows were neglected in the daily distribution of food.

The twelve apostles did not get offended or defensive because of the complaint, neither were they dismissive. They recognized that a spirit-filled believer should never be discriminatory based on race as the blood of Jesus is a uniting force that has brought all nations together, including Jews and Greeks, white and black, Latino and Asia.

And so the twelve apostles appointed seven spirit-filled believers to administer over food in dealing with the issue. The bible says the word of God spread, and the number of the disciples multiplied. When we are deliberate in fixing disunity in the Body of Christ, a multiplying effect occurs in harvest. "Behold, how good and how pleasant it is for brethren to dwell together in unity!"(Psalm 133:1)

God values diversity. The Holy Spirit chose to come at Pentecost because people from every nation under the earth gathered at Pentecost, aside from the evangelistic strategy behind this (Acts 2).

Jesus was a Jew. He was deliberate in including a non-Jew, a Canaanite, among His cabinet ministers, His twelve apostles (Mathew 10:4).

I heard in passing someone giving the explanation for why when it's a white pastor, the congregation is generally white. When it's a black pastor, or Latino, or Asian, the congregation reflects the respective racial identity of the pastor. And here is the explanation that the person gives: "each attracts its kind" or "each according to its kind".

I know that the only times that expression was used in the bible was in Genesis and Ezekiel. And it was used for animals. "Each attracts its kind" was used for Noah's animals or for Ezekiel's fish. We are not animals. We are human beings, created in the precious image of God.

Paul was a Jew. But He attracted mostly non-Jews. And if each must attract its kind to promote diversity and prevent racial division in the church, then we need to challenge ourselves to take deliberate actions so that each will attract its kind.

As a white pastor, be deliberate in prayerfully seeking out people of other colors: Latino, Asian, Black, and African- American, to be part of your leadership team just the way Jesus did in seeking out the Canaanite for His leadership team.

As a Latino, or Asian or African-American or African Black pastor, be deliberate in prayerfully seeking out white people to be in your leadership team. You pray to God:

> *"Father in heaven, I know it is your good*
> *pleasure to have people of all nations*

*worship you as your servant John records
in the book of revelation.*

*I want to have people of all nations worship
You in this congregation since it brings
delight to you.*

*I ask for your wisdom, direction and favor
as I step out in doing this for the sake of
your Holy name and so that your kingdom
is always reflected in this congregation."*

Such sincere prayers that touches His heart God does not ignore. He may even have a plan for your congregation different from what you are asking for. But He will really appreciate your sincerity and concern for His kingdom and He will bless you for it.

When the kingdom of God that values diversity is actively pursued by the church, the church will be better positioned in dealing with the issue of division in the nation. We are THE Light of the world. No other light.

A kingdom divided against itself cannot stand. I have even heard that some Christian leader said unity and racial parity within the church cannot be dealt with while we are on earth, but that this will happen only when we get to heaven.

Here is my response to this line of thought. Then we do not need to be praying for the kingdom of God to come on the earth, to our churches. We should not be inviting heaven to come on the earth. We should wait till we get to heaven.

The reason is because the heavenly kingdom of God that John describes in the scriptures is very diverse and of course, the passengers on the journey to it, which is the focus of this book, will be very diverse. We can as well try and start getting used to one another before the time comes.

Again, the kingdom we often pray for and invite to the earth cannot change its identity in order to accommodate us. We need to be prepared to receive it because it is very racially diverse.

I was told the other time that a people of color joined a church, and when they joined the choir team, the team full of white people complained to the pastor they were not comfortable with black people and they began to leave one by one. They need salvation to qualify for the final flight.

I was told that the pastor stood his ground, perhaps, because of some other reasons given that I do not want to share here. But as a result the church was better for it.

Today's management science indicates that a more diverse workplace is more productive and more prosperous. I suppose this idea was stolen from the bible by those who do not belong to the Light of Jesus or perhaps was applied by kingdom people for life, if godliness refuses to embrace it.

Today's management science indicates that a more diverse workplace is more productive and more prosperous. I suppose this idea was stolen from the bible

Speaking of anointing, it may be difficult to be blessed through the anointing of someone to whom we are racially biased. They may even be the prerogative purpose carriers as I describe in this book, for our specific situations.

They may be transmitting and transponding signals for God's healing and deliverance. But as long as our faith reception for the signals is closed because of our biases, we may be limiting what God wants to do in our lives.

Jesus could not do many mighty miracles in His hometown Nazareth because, as the bible says, His people were too familiar with His humble beginning as a mere carpenter's son whose parents and siblings are just down the street. And of course Nazareth was stereotyped as a place nothing good comes from, talk less of the Messiah.

Even when they saw the miracles He performed, they wondered where He got the power from and were offended that He was undeserving to be able to perform wonders. Mark's gospel records that Jesus could not do many mighty miracles there. Notice this: He "could not", even as much as He would have wanted to.

Black Angels

All the angels that I have seen appear to me in visions, are black. This means that the celestial bodies are deliberate in wearing an earthly tent that is black and they are comfortable with it. We should quit making excuses for our actions and inactions for things we know are dear to God's heart!

Paul always went with the locals in most, if not all of his missionary journeys. In fact, Peter, the leader of the church and of the apostles, confirmed that God does not discriminate between Jews and non-Jews when He saw the Holy Spirit fall on all the household of Cornelius.

And when Peter reneged on this conviction, trying to be politically correct in his refusal to publicly identify with non-Jews in Antioch, Paul rebuked him and all those who joined him sharply for their hypocrisy, in the presence of all (Galatians 2).

That God not only created diverse nations and colors, but that He created them also for His own pleasure and He delights in seeing them together in worshipping Him, cannot be over-emphasized.

John the Beloved confirmed this in the book of revelation when he saw a great multitude in heaven, which no one could number from all nations, tribes, peoples, and tongues worshipping and praising God (Revelations 7:9).

A pastor, spiritual leader or a church that goes out of their way to seek out people of other nations and color and is deliberate in putting things in place within their congregation to ensure diversity is sustained, is literarily inviting the heavenly kingdom that John describes here and they will be blessed for it.

I remember how a Reverend in rural Alberta narrated his story of how he prayed and was seeking out black African Christians that could come to his community to speak to the youth who think Jesus was just a historical figure and that He was meant for the Jews only.

He was at an event when he was hoping that his wishes and prayers would come through. And just a short while later, he got what he prayed and longed for.

He ran into some friends of mine and he arranged to have us speak about Jesus at a youth camp. After the event, he confirmed that the spiritual atmosphere changed, praise God. He prayed for it and was deliberate. He got it.

I remember some time ago, a guest pastor was speaking at a church where I served. He was a white pastor. I was on my knees as we were worshipping. The Holy Spirit said to me: "How about you have a joint service with his church".

Just about two minutes later, the guest pastor said the same thing: "I am sensing in my spirit that we need to have a joint service with your church."

The guest pastor was so deliberate in wanting to obey the Lord to the point he offered to be the one playing the piano for worship while my pastor will take the microphone to preach during the joint service. I immediately raised my hands to confirm that I received the same word from the Lord two minutes before.

These last days, God is calling for kingdom-minded leaders who will tell their congregation "today, we are going to the church down the street to have a combined service with them. These are people that want to practice the kingdom of God on earth and they will be blessed for it.

Forgiver in-Chief

Our good Lord Jesus is the Forgiver in-Chief. He expects us to be like Him. I remember some time ago I was given opportunity to speak somewhere about an outreach program my ministry was organizing. I saw someone in the group who had not treated me right.

I saw this as an opportunity to communicate my forgiveness. So I looked for something good about them and it was the first thing I said when I was given the microphone.

After the program, someone that knew about the issue between me and that fellow approached me, saying they were surprised but equally applauded me for doing that in spite of what this fellow has done.

The point is this, anyone who is waiting or expecting Jesus to return for the final flight must learn to be like Jesus, the Forgiver in-Chief.

The number of times requested by Jesus we ought to forgive someone who has sinned against us is seventy times seven. This number indicates completeness and it is limitless. It indicates we need a bucket full of forgiveness so we can hand it out when the need arises. Before people offend or betray you, Jesus knows. Jesus knew that Judas was going to betray Him.

Let me recount two examples of this that further demonstrates the Lord's omniscience. In a dream, I saw a former colleague of mine with whom I worked at the University of Alberta, after a long time.

I saw him in the location where we once worked together. And I asked him and called his name, a much younger fellow, "what are you doing here?" He answered me that he was back.

And I woke up from the dream. The next morning, after spending some time in my office, I felt the need to go out for a brief walk. As I stepped out, less than half a block away, I ran into someone I knew that I had not seen for at least a year. It was the lively young man I saw in my dream the night before.

As I wasn't prepared for the surprise occasion, I let the cat out of the bag: "Oh look at you, [...] (I mentioned his name). What are you doing here? I saw you in my dream last night." If I was prepared, I wouldn't have been quick to tell him I saw him in a dream as this unnecessarily raised his curiosity.

But notice his response to me "Oga Josh, am back for my master's o. At the U of A o". Exactly the exchange with him in my dream the night before. Jesus was using the dream to demonstrate His omniscience to me, and of course to you. He knew what I would do the next day.

Jesus knew how I would feel the next day in the office to the point I would step out for a brief walk, something that was not a habit for me to do.

He knew I would run into my former colleague and He knew exactly what our conversation would be like. Jesus is all-seeing and all-knowing. So quit worrying that someone would offend or betray you.

Sometimes they might even lie about the situation in a way that upsets you the more; you have an obligation to forgive. You have a purpose to fulfill and a glorious journey with Jesus that you are waiting for. Ponder on this journey that will mark an end to all forms of offense and hurt against you.

In another dream, Jesus showed me something painful someone else would do to me, a fellow believer. I woke up from the dream with an usual chest pain. When I woke up, Jesus said to me, quoting from Hebrews 3:3 "Look unto Jesus, the Apostle and the High Priest of your faith."

About two months later, it happened exactly the way I saw it in my dream. And the Lord told me that is what He was showing me in the dream two months earlier.

One morning, I lay on the carpet in my living room. Jesus said this to me: "Joshua, you have the capacity to forgive." Then I looked around me, asking Lord, "who have I not forgiven?" Little did I know that the reminder was meant for an offense on the way.

Same day in the evening, I received a call from a believer. Getting to know the actual reason for their call after 45 minutes left me disappointed.

As believers, we need a bucket full of forgiveness that we will need to hand out as offenses come in. As long as we remain in this imperfect world, forgiveness is like water, an essential commodity for living. We also need to be mindful to avoid being the cause for offenses.

CHAPTER 15- PROTEIN NEEDED IN CHURCH

Another vital thing that we need to get us ready for the coming of Jesus and the final flight is what I call protein for the Body of Christ. We are no doubts in a harvest season for perishing souls. It is the last harvest. But it is what I call the penultimate revival. The last revival, as I describe later, will happen after the final flight.

Protein is needed in church in this penultimate revival to bring in the last harvest. Protein is needed by the laborers in the harvest field so they have all that is needed to harvest souls. In nutritional science, protein as a category of nutrient is given as the most essential for body building and growth.

There are five spiritual nutrients required by the church, the Body of Christ, in order to fulfill its purpose. Each of these five spiritual nutrients have a distinct food source for you to get the nutrients in adequate measures. The apostle Paul identifies these food sources in his description of the five-fold ministries. See how he describes them:

"And he gave some, apostles; and some, prophets; and some, evangelists; and some, pastors and teachers;

> *for the perfecting of the saints, for the work*
> *of the ministry, for the edifying of the body*
> *of Christ:"*

Jesus has determined that for His church, which is His Body, to be adequately nourished and supplied with required nutrients, its food must come from 5 distinct food sources identified as the five-fold ministry.

As they are listed in the scripture above, they are the ministry of the apostles, prophets, evangelists, pastors and teachers. This means that a church cannot afford not to have all of these in required measures.

It means that a church cannot just be feeding from the apostle food source and neglect that of the prophet. Neither should a church be fed with the pastoral food at the expense of the teacher or the evangelist food source. It is my opinion that the evangelist ministry is the protein ministry for the Body of Christ.

I describe the apostle and the prophet as carbohydrates and fats respectively. The apostle comes with a kingdom message, a lot of carbs for the listeners about what God is doing or intends to do from a kingdom perspective and he gets the people excited.

The prophet brings the presence of God into people's personal situation or a nation's situation. The pastor and the teacher provide in small measures a bit of all the nutrients but mostly vitamins that help retain what has been consumed. And all these are energy-giving food sources.

But the evangelist is the nutritional source for protein among these ministries that drives body-building and numerical growth for kingdom expansion. A church without the evangelist's protein in adequate measure is suffering from spiritual kwashiorkor – which is a deficiency of protein. It may be fat on the apostle's feeding or the prophet, it stops growing both in the physical and spiritual realms without the protein. It may even be a large church, it stops growing without the protein evangelist.

Now a pastor for instance can operate the activity of the evangelist. In fact, Paul instructs the young pastor Timothy to do the work of an evangelist (2 Timothy 4:5). On the one hand, Paul was giving this instruction to Timothy knowing that Timothy already has his hands full.

As a young leader, Timothy needed to take care of the controversies, build the church, to study to show himself approved unto God, rightly dividing the word of the truth and endure hardship through this whole process. In spite of having his hands already full , Timothy is given another charge to do the work of an evangelist in his pastoral role (2 Timothy 4:5).

With this charge, Paul was indicating to Timothy he should not be too caught up with the needed pastoral work to the point he neglects the major earthly role of the church. A church without the protein evangelist is already losing its heartbeat, because evangelism is the heartbeat of God.

Increasingly you will see workers in the Body of Christ identifying as pastors, prophets or apostles. Little or no emphasis is placed on the pivotal role played by the ministry of the evangelist in kingdom building and expansion. The same fate is suffered by the teaching ministry.

I am not calling for recognition of the title of an evangelist for believers as this in itself leads to a separate issue of the pride of life. Neither am I talking about the believers that are actively engaged in the work of evangelism. Every believer of Jesus should.

What am talking about here is the ministry of the evangelist, called and ordained by God to teach and equip the body of Christ for the work of the ministry as the scriptures intend it. It is our job to be sensitive to the leading of the Holy Spirit to identify them within our local churches. This does not stop the pastor from doing the work of the evangelist as Paul directed Timothy.

But remember, Timothy himself was an evangelist taking up a needed role as a pastor to fix things. If there is no evangelist within your local church, look for them elsewhere to feed your congregation with protein.

Some churches are increasingly being turned into a fast food restaurant where the spiritual leader is always looking to preach on what the members want- blessings, favor, prosperity and the likes. Only sometimes the evangelist protein is inserted into these.

"The winner takes it all" is a predisposition of both sides of the spirit realm

These are good things and they are part of the benefits of the kingdom of God. But they do not define the main earthly purpose of the church. Jesus said my house shall be a house of prayers. When His disciples requested of Him how to pray, Jesus said, "this then is how you should pray".

The word "How" indicates the "manner", "method" model or "pattern", "the order" in which we should pray.

And He goes further to list this order. First, *"Our Father in heaven"* – that is acknowledge who He is and which father you are talking to. Second, "hallowed be your name" – that is praise and worship Him".

Now, pay attention to the very first request, before any other requests, Jesus is asking us to make when we pray: Third, *"Your Kingdom come. Your will be done on earth as it is in heaven."* (Mathew 6:8-13)

In heaven, everyone is in submission to God and under the Lordship of Jesus. It is not so here on earth. This is not a lesson on prayer. What am saying here is that with this prayer, Jesus gave His mission statement for the church, and He repeated this mission statement just before His departure from the world. He gave a revelation on what is of prior and utmost importance to God when we gather in church – that is the expansion of His Kingdom on earth to the point everyone on earth is in submission to God.

Any church gathering with this kingdom expansionist goal as its main purpose, falls within not only of the main purpose of the church, but also of the Lord's ultimate purpose for the gathering as can be seen in this scripture.

In verse 33 of the same scripture, Jesus reinforces this mission statement for our gathering and the priority we should accord it – *"But seek first the kingdom of God and His righteousness, and all these things shall be added to you."* I believe the 80-20 rule applies here. Eighty percent of our kingdom activities should be for this goal, while the remaining 20 percent should be for other things.

I told you earlier in this book how I preached that a focus on this divine purpose attracts favor, wealth and blessing from God and how Jesus appeared to me the next day showing me a piece of diamond with a thumbs up. Jesus says in this scripture, "seek first the kingdom of God".

It's interesting He didn't say we should seek other things after seeking the Kingdom of God. Seeking first the kingdom automatically attracts blessing.

I was so delighted recently to watch a pastor devote her entire message to the teaching on evangelism. Such is rare these days. It was not a large congregation. But my delight was doubled when I saw a sizable number of new believers being prepared for water baptism in this rather small-size church.

Save All. Not Some

Speaking of expanding the kingdom through the message of the gospel and everything good that it comes with, I have noticed a counterproductive narrative among

Christians on this. I hear people pray and ask the Holy Spirit how many people He wants to save at a meeting.

The bible says that God desires that ALL human beings be saved and come to the knowledge of the truth. Well I say that's God's mission statement when it comes to redemption for humanity. ALL, without exception. Every offspring of Adam and Eve is a target for redemption. It's a bid for total recall of the human species. The Holy Spirit operates based on the words He Himself authored in the bible.

Yes, He wants to save all from sin. So when we pray, we need to pray God's desire, His mission statement. That's why Jesus says we should pray that His kingdom come and that His will be done on earth, as it is in heaven. I mentioned earlier that the will of God in heaven is that everyone is in total submission to Him as Lord.

That's what He wants to do on the earth with our participation. So as believers, we need to always pray in line with God's word. When we pray for salvation for our family, we pray that ALL without exception is saved. The same with our cities, states, provinces, countries and continents.

"The winner takes it all" is a unique predisposition of the realm of the spirit, even on both sides. For instance, in Nebuchadnezzar's Babylon, only 4 Hebrew children did not comply with the king's decree to bow down to the graven image.

Yet, in an empire of perhaps hundreds of millions of people, the king was still not satisfied. He demanded hundred percent compliance with his decree. The same with God, He wants hundred percent of Adam's seed saved.

That's why as an evangelist, even after preaching and hundreds of thousands or millions of people are saved, you should still not be satisfied as long as there are Adam's seed that are yet to be saved.

After a successful crusade with millions saved, the co-guest at your hotel room or the co-passenger on the flight home is Adam's seed. They need salvation too. It might be the only time you will see them. It's a total recall of Adam's seed corrupted with Satan's seed of sin.

But unlike the kingdom of darkness, God will not apply the instrument of force to achieve His desire. God will only apply the bait of love so humanity can willingly choose to worship Him. That is class!

Don't Leave it to the Sales Man

Imagine you want to buy an essential product from a company. You enter their office and by coincidence you run into the CEO. The CEO tells you he needs to go for a board meeting, asking you to wait for the sales man. The vice president does the same thing. The accountant tells you they need to balance the books and that the sales man should be on his way.

The hiring manager is also busy training new staff. You are left with the option to leave for another company with the essential product. If it's the only company with the essential product, you are denied access to the product because the company staff are too busy with activities to respond to sales.

They leave the job of making a sale, which is critical to business growth, to the sales man. I'm sure you will know that the shareholders of the company will not be happy to know of your experience. They will be very concerned.

Sadly, we see the same attitude of "leave it to the sales man" in churches today. Many in church feel it's the work of the evangelist to make the sales, to preach and win lost souls to the kingdom. Some will say my calling is to lead worship, to be a pastor, an usher, choir etc.

Notwithstanding our position or activities in the church, all of us are responsible for making the sales to reach lost souls with the gospel of the kingdom. It's all about the sales that drives growth in the kingdom company. The heavenly shareholders are watching and waiting for us to earnestly pursue this goal.

Be Transactional- You Have Been Cheated

The apostle Paul in the bible said that he put his body under subjection so that after preaching to many, he himself will not be disqualified, for example, from the final flight (1 Corinthians 1:27).

What I make of this is that the preaching mode puts us on alert to be careful, be ready and be reminded of the hope that believers have as we preach to others about the kingdom.

To be ready for the final flight, you need an activity sanctioned by God that will constantly remind you of this soon-to-happen glorious event. That activity is preaching the kingdom to others as a habit.

One way you can do this is to be transactional. The world we live in is transactional and time is the currency used in the process. Our interaction with work, school, and market places are transactional.

We always exchange something for the other. Unfortunately, our body and soul are almost always the only parties to these transactions. Our spirit, which is the real us, is not given a chance.

Our new spirit in Christ has been designed to negotiate other new spirits for the soul of man through the spread of the gospel. But we do not allow it to be part of our daily transactions. For example, we buy and sell, we make payment or exchange information with others daily.

These transactions are done by our body and soul, hence we have been cheated too many times, without our spirit's involvement. When we buy or sell something, our soul and body have given something away.

Balanced Trade

To be transactional, we need to demand something for our spirit in return. Some years ago, my family and I bought a vehicle from the dealership. After a couple of weeks, I realized my soul and body had given something away in that transaction.

And I felt my spirit needed to get something back in return. So, I went back to the dealership with a bunch of gospel cards, requesting the sales manager to allow my cards in their shop for a while for their customers to pick up. He did. And I saw the cards still on their desk for a while and some were picked up.

It was at this point I thought I broke even in the transaction in which we purchased the car. Sometimes you go to the grocery or clothing store and you buy items on sale. You feel you have gotten the best deal. No, you have been cheated! The real you is your spirit. It is your body and soul that got the goods on sale.

To break even, you need to let your spirit benefit from the transaction. You have bought something with your body and soul. Your spirit needs to sell something in return to make the trade balanced and fair.

The only transaction your spirit makes with the world around you is what the Holy Spirit of God does and asks him to. That is to make fishers of men through the spread of the gospel fishing net. It is then you are making the best use of the world system to your advantage.

Therefore, the next time you go for groceries, be sure to tell the cashier Jesus loves her to the point He shed His blood for her redemption from sin to God. You have earned the right and the audience for your spirit to present the gospel in exchange for the purchase that your soul and body have just made. It's transactional. But don't be cheated anymore!

You Are a Fire-Fighter

I hear believers wait for the Lord to open doors for the gospel. No, it's our responsibility to open the doors - physical and spiritual. Some doors will never be opened until we open it.

The psalmist recognized this, hence he says *"Lift up your heads, o you gates! And be lifted up, you everlasting doors! And the King of glory shall come in" (Psalm 24:7).*

Like the psalmist, we need to command an opening to the spiritual and physical doors blocking the king of glory and his gospel of eternal life from reaching the lost. After commanding in prayers, we need to go open the physical doors.

> *The psalmist isn't asking the Lord to open the doors and gates! He commands them to open.*

If you believe the gospel of the eternal kingdom is indispensable and an urgent need for all of humanity, then I want you to do this for me briefly: picture yourself as a firefighter standing outside of the door to a house engulfed in flames. In that house is a baby in need of an urgent rescue. The baby represents the helpless state of the lost.

As a believer, that makes you a firefighter. Break the damn door! The disciple Jude seems to understand this principle, hence he says, "save others by snatching them from the fire..." (Jude 1:23).

Missionaries in adversarial territories seem to understand this principle when they break man-made rules to allow the flow of living water through the fire-hose of the eternal gospel of Jesus the King of glory, to quench the fire surrounding the lost that need rescue and bring them to the kingdom.

Yes, it is the believer's duty to open the spiritual and physical doors. The psalmist agrees with this. Speaking through the Holy Spirit, he says "Lift up your heads oh you gates! And be lifted up, you everlasting doors! And the king of glory shall come in" Psalm 24:7.

In persistence, he repeats in chorus the same command in verse 9. The psalmist isn't asking the Lord to open the doors and gates! He commands them to open. Child of God, in these last days, make it a duty to prayerfully open the spiritual doors and physically open the doors to the hearts of the lost, the cities and nations. And the gospel of peace, joy, love and everlasting life through Jesus Christ, will go into the hearts of people.

Sometimes people feel the evangelist must demonstrate healing power to preach. But salvation is the actual demonstration of the Holy Spirit's power. When the gospel is preached, and a sinner repents and is born again, that's the greatest healing miracle because the old spirit of man is exchanged for a brand new one. The soul and the body that need healing are gradually conditioned to follow the lead of the new spirit.

And in the order of superiority in the tripartite make-up of mankind, the spirit comes first, for we are first spirit-beings, then the soul, then the body, which is our earthly tent. A focus on healing of the body first, as opposed to salvation, is already a miscarriage of kingdom priority purpose.

When a sinner wants to repent, there is movement in their body. The mouth says the confession prayers; the hand sometimes is lifted. The eyes are sometimes closed with tears flowing down giving physical evidence to people around that their soulish, emotional being has been touched by the gospel message resulting in the decision to repent.

Now that the soul has yielded to the evading force of the power of the gospel enabled by the Holy Spirit, their spirit undergoes a complete conversion and becomes new. Salvation of sinners is the greatest 'demonstration' of His power. In fact, salvation is the "demonstration" of the Holy Spirit's power. Other things like healing, are physical "manifestations" of His power.

Writing to the Corinthian church in the bible, Paul says *"My message and my preaching were not with wise and persuasive words, but with a demonstration of the Spirit's power, so that your faith might not rest on human wisdom, but on God's power." (1Corinthians 2:4-5).*

Later in the 12th chapter, he writes to distinguish that "to each one manifestations of the Spirit is given for the common good" (v.7). And the gifts of healing are listed as one of these manifestations.

You see now. For salvation, Holy Spirit demonstrates His power. For healing, He manifests His power. Don't get me wrong. I believe in healing miracles. I have witnessed people being healed and I have been miraculously healed myself.

> *In fact, salvation is the "demonstration" of the Holy Spirit's power. Other things like healing, are physical "manifestations" of His power.*

Gospel Attracts Healing

Preaching of the gospel of the kingdom and Jesus as the way to that kingdom automatically attracts healing. The manifestations of the gifts of healing happen more intensely where there is a mission for the gospel or it is being preached. Virtually all the miraculous healing recorded in the bible that the disciples performed were performed when they were actively engaged in the spread of the gospel.

Let me share with you another word of wisdom the Lord gave me regarding the very first healing miracle performed by the disciples after Jesus' departure and after the Holy Spirit arrived at Pentecost.

The first healing account recorded in Acts chapter 3 is often misinterpreted. I have heard many a preacher say that the healing of the crippled man by Peter in this scripture happened because it was at the hour of prayer as Peter and John were heading to the temple at the hour of prayer. No doubt, a lot of powerful and good things happen at the hour of prayer. But the miracle did not happen because it was the hour of prayer.

> *But the miracle did not happen because it was the hour of prayer.*

The Lord opened my eyes to see why it happened. Yes, Peter and John were going to the temple at the hour of prayer. But they were not going for prayers. It was a Judaism prayer. Peter and John were followers of the new Way – Jesus. Imagine two spirit-filled believers armed with the gospel of truth going to a Muslim mosque where a fellow Christian had recently been killed for their belief.

Peter and John were going to the same temple where those who crucified their Lord and Savior pray. They were embarking on one of the most dangerous evangelistic missionary journeys. And the Lord Jesus whom they believe and now preach has been put on the spot in which He has to prove to the crucifers that He is alive.

The crippled beggar neither asked for healing, nor did he have the faith for it. He asked for money. None of these matters to God. Suddenly, the Holy Spirit released the manifestation of the gift of faith on Peter. Peter was ignited for a pacesetting supernatural moment that would characterize the Acts of the Apostles.

"Look at us!" Peter said to the man born crippled. And as he looks at them, expecting to get something from them,

> *"Then Peter said, Silver and gold have I none; but such as I have give I thee: In the name of Jesus Christ of Nazareth*
>
> *rise up and walk. And he took him by the right hand and lifted him up: and immediately his feet and ankle bones received strength. (Acts 3:6-7)*

Walking and jumping, the beggar went with them to the temple to the surprise of all who knew him. Solomon's Colonnade, the outer court of the temple, became a temporary church and it was opened up to Peter and John who preached the new way to those who are still in amazement of what happened. And about 2,000 more believers were added to the disciples.

Even the rulers of the temple who opposed everything about the Way of Jesus acknowledge that it was a "notable miracle".

Here is how the Holy Spirit describes this miracle in explaining why it was recorded in the bible that the man was over 4o years old – another word of wisdom from the good Lord:

> *"The miracle was a paradigm shift. No one had been miraculously healed at such age since the time of the prophets".*

Indeed, any activity tailored by believers for the expansion of the kingdom is a magnet to attract the supernatural for healing miracles.

And according to the Lord's own words to me, when it comes to healing and manifestations of the Holy Spirit in these last days, "the glory of the latter days shall surpass the former".

I know without a doubt that at the mention of the name of Jesus by His believers, the blind have received their sight, the crippled have walked, the sick have been made well and the dead have been raised to life.

All these will happen in greater frequencies than ever before in these last days. And they are already happening. Miraculous healing should not become so commercialized and prized to the point we restrict it to the five ministry areas and since the evangelist and teacher are relegated to the background, we now see such appellations as "healing evangelist".

Every born again child of God should seek to position himself or herself as a conduit for the release of God's miraculous healing power. Manifestations are meant to promote belief in the Lord Jesus and advance kingdom expansion.

Jesus is very clear on this kingdom purpose even when He miraculously healed the sick. Some desperate friends of a bedridden man brought the man to Jesus and lowered him down through the roof of the house where Jesus was surrounded by people.

> *Every born again child of God should seek to position himself or herself as a conduit for the release of God's miraculous healing power*

Before Jesus healed the man, notice what He said to him: "When Jesus saw their faith, He said to the man, 'Friend, your sins are forgiven" (Luke 5:17-39).

In addition to wanting to indicate to people around that He had the power to forgive sin on the earth, Jesus was also sending a message here that the forgiveness of sin, the salvation needed to qualify for the final flight to the kingdom of God is of prior importance to Him and God.

Hence, while applauding their unyielding faith, He was nudging them to direct their effort towards seeking Him for the forgiveness of sins. Experiencing or witnessing miraculous healing does not translate to belief in Jesus or repentance from sin.

Notice how Jesus pronounced judgment on three cities in which He demonstrated His miraculous healing power and yet they did not believe in Him:

> *"Woe to you, Chorazin! Woe to you, Bethsaida! For if the mighty works which were done in you had been done in Tyre and Sidon, they would have repented long ago in sackcloth and ashes.*
>
> *But I say to you, it will be more tolerable for Tyre and Sidon in the Day of Judgment than for you.*
>
> *And you, Capernaum, who are exalted to heaven, will be brought down to Hades; for if the mighty works which were done in you*
>
> *had been done in Sodom, it would have remained until this day. But I say to you that it shall be more tolerable for the land of Sodom in the Day of Judgment than for you." (Mathew 11:20-24").*

Through the mighty miraculous works, Capernaum was even exalted to heaven, which means they had open visions to the kingdom of God, yet they did not believe. These pronouncements are profound.

When the healing anointing is in operation, we should make it our own duty to steward it towards belief in Jesus and kingdom expansion. We should be deliberate in inviting recipients of these healing miracles and the witnesses to it, to come to repentance, believe in Jesus and make a commitment to serve Jesus the Healer.

We should nudge those in the atmosphere for healing to make a commitment to proclaim Jesus for the rest of their lives. Healing miracles, signs and wonders and prophecies that are not stewarded towards kingdom expansion express God's kindness. They are meaningless if they do not fully convey the reason for this kindness, which is to expand His kingdom to the recipients and witnesses.

We always call for revival and special outpouring of the power of the Holy Spirit. When it happens, it happens for the sole purpose of kingdom expansion. We should first be prepared to harvest souls for the kingdom in preparation for the revival we yearn for.

The apostles in the bible understood this. The first revival happened at Pentecost with the arrival of the Holy Spirit. Peter stewarded this by preaching the gospel of the kingdom and inviting those around to repent and turn to Jesus as Lord.

About three thousand new believers were added to Jesus' followers as a result of this. And if you have been a recipient of miraculous healing from Jesus, know this for sure, the hand of the creator God touched you when it happened. When the woman with the medical condition of hemorrhage for 12 years touched Jesus and received her healing instantly, Jesus said, someone touched "me" and as a result, power came out of Him.

> *God has humbled and loved on you with His kindness. The intent of this touch is so you know He is a tangible God and so that you can tell others to come to Him for the rest of your life*

The power of God is His right hand. The Psalmist in the bible says the right hand of God is majestic in power (psalm 118:16). Any miraculous healing comes from the right hand of God through Jesus. So, you have been touched by the hand of God. Like Capernaum, you were exalted to heaven when it happened.

God has humbled and loved on you with His kindness. The intent of this touch is so you know He is a tangible God and so that you can tell others to come to Him for the rest of your life. After healing the 10 lepers, only one of them came back to thank Jesus. Jesus said were there not 10 lepers that were healed and only one came back?

The bible says that Jesus made the leper that came back whole in his body. This means he restored his shortened fingers and restored all the body parts that leprosy had taken away. If you appreciate His healing by following him, in addition to the physical healing on your body, He will give you a glorified body when He returns for the final flight.

CHAPTER 16 THE THIRD CREATION EVENT

The Holy Spirit gave me some profound revelations that He wants me to share with you regarding the prophetic things that will happen at the coming of Jesus. I have shared with you about the final flight, the resurrection of the dead, explanation of some of the controversies around this subject and things we need to do to prepare for Jesus' return.

Now in this chapter, let's look at another significant event that will accompany the coming of Jesus and the prophetic insight given by Him.

> *"For the Lord Himself will descend from heaven with a shout, with the voice of an archangel, and with the trumpet of God. And the dead in Christ will rise first.*
>
> *Then we who are alive and remain shall be caught up together with them in the clouds to meet the Lord in the air. And thus we shall always be with the Lord" (1 Thessalonians 4:16-17)*

I call it the Third Creation Event. I put this in context. The first creation event that concerns humans was in genesis when God created Adam and Eve. The second creation event was in the New Testament with Jesus giving a new spirit to all those who believe in Him – they are born again.

Then the third creation event is the creation of a new body, a glorious body for all those who are born again, or the saints. This great creation event will happen almost at once for all the saints when Jesus returns for the final flight. Jesus said to me that this will happen in sequential order with the rest of the events surrounding the coming of Jesus. Let's go for a smooth ride on this.

The scripture above identifies three separate events that will happen with Jesus in the sky when he descends from heaven for the final flight. They are (1) a shout from the Lord Himself, (2) the voice of an archangel, and (3) the trumpet of God. In other words, Jesus will announce His arrival in three separate formats.

On Friday December 15, 2017, between 2 and 4am, Jesus told me in an open vision that the shout from the Lord is to declare victory over death. He said the archangel appearing with Jesus is a Seraph. I am still trying to understand what this means and why it's a Seraph.

But pay attention to this. He said the voice coming from the archangel will call forth the spoken repentance or confession prayers of every believer to create a resurrected, glorious body for them. And then He linked this up to John chapter 1: the Word (Jesus) was and became flesh.

The Lord also pointed me to Romans 10: 9-10:

> *"that if you confess with your mouth the Lord Jesus and believe in your heart that God has raised Him from the dead, you will be saved.*

For with the heart one believes unto
righteousness, and with the mouth
confession is made unto salvation "

Confession is evidence of your belief that Jesus is Lord, that He died and shed His blood for the remission of your sins and that God raised Him up from the dead, signifying resurrection and eternal life for all who believe in Him.

The confessionary evidence may not be important to the preacher. It may not even be important to you. But it is important to God. It is important to his angels who work hard to keep records of every word spoken. Jesus, God, the Holy Spirit are omniscient – all knowing.

The angels on the other hand, are not omniscient. They cannot read your mind to know the state of your belief. As far as the angels are concerned, God accepts you as His own only when you confess that you are a sinner, you ask Him to remit your sin because Jesus paid for it with His blood and you confess that God raised Him up from the dead and that Jesus is your Lord and savior.

That is important to the angels to include you in the inventory of God's holy saints. That's why the scripture in Romans 10:10 above presents a 2-part test for membership in God's big family: "For with the heart one believes unto righteousness (unto Jesus) and with the mouth confession is made unto salvation (saved because angels hear your confession).

The confessionary evidence may not be important to the preacher. It may not even be important to you. But it is important to God. It is important to his angels who work hard to keep records of every word spoken

God included this confession piece in the scripture because He has assigned this critical piece of work to His trusted holy angels to carry out the process of your salvation. You cannot believe and not confess.

Writing to the Corinthian church, Paul says *"And since we have the same spirit of faith, according to what is written, "I believed and therefore I spoke, we also believe and therefore speak," (2 Corinthians 4:13).*

Confession for salvation is not only needed now to be certified a true child of God. As I describe above from what the precious Holy Spirit revealed to me, it is also needed for the creation of glorious bodies for those who have been qualified by Jesus to embark on the most important journey – the final flight.

The Seraph, the archangel with his voice will call forth the confession you have made and that is how you will have your glorious or glorified body that defies gravity, for the flight.

Your confession is the evidence for God's Holy angels who work hard to keep records and it will be needed to create your glorified body for the final flight

If you are a preacher or a pastor or an evangelist, the first thing you want to do is to get the people to believe in the gospel and subsequently respond with confession.

Sharing of the gospel is not complete without a request for confession. Again, I repeat this, our gospel message is not complete without a request for confession.

It is complete whether or not people confess as long as you have made a request for it.

And if anyone comes to God for forgiveness of sin through the sacrifice of blood that Jesus made, God is bound to forgive because His justice system is made up of this blood. The blood of Jesus is very powerful.

The gospel is an invitation to a provision for redemption that was produced, sealed, signed and made available to all of mankind on Calvary Cross. Our job as preachers in partnership with the Holy Spirit is to explain this complete package and deliver it to all and sundry.

When it is accepted through belief, evidence of its acceptance needs to be made through confession. It is this confessionary evidence that the angels need to record and take to the file room in heaven. The church is a place where confession should be one of the primary goals for each service.

In God's spiritual law court, whenever an argument is made using the blood of Jesus, a strong case is made for acquittal of the sinner

Let me explain this. After aggressively dispersing the buyers and sellers who turned the temple into a market place, Jesus quoted the prophets Jeremiah and Isaiah. *"[...]* *"It is written, 'My house shall be called a house of prayer, but you have made it a 'den of thieves.'" (Mathew 21:13).*

A house of prayer is a house of worship and communication between God and man. If the church is a house of prayer, then it is a house of confession. Confession is in two parts depending on the person concerned.

First, it involves a person acknowledging who they are (a sinner), what they have done (sinned). Second, it involves acknowledging what God has done to save them from sin (Jesus shed His blood on the Cross). And asking for forgiveness for sins because of this sacrifice, making a declaration to repent (turn away) from sin (Satan's mark), to God.

> *In God's spiritual law court, whenever an argument is made using the blood of Jesus, a strong and the only legitimate case for the acquittal of the sinner-criminal has been made*

Second, confession involves acknowledging and declaring who God is to me now (Jesus my Lord and savior). Making Jesus Lord and savior is a determination not to go back to sin as we are no longer slaves to sin. But slaves unto righteousness because Jesus is now Lord over us, not sin or Satan. Halleluiah!

This line of thought that confession should perhaps be the primary goal for every church service or gathering is reinforced by the Lord Jesus himself when He taught His disciples how to pray. Jesus said, *"In this manner"*, meaning in this pattern, method, order, *"therefore, pray"*:

> *Our Father in heaven, Hallowed be Your name. Your Kingdom come. Your will be done on earth as it is in heaven. Give us this our daily bread.*
>
> *And forgive us our debts, As we forgive our Debtors. And do not lead us into temptation, But deliver us from the evil one.*
>
> *For Yours is the kingdom and the power and the glory forever. Amen. (Mathew 6:9-13)*

Notice the order of prayers here: *"Our Father in heaven* (identify and acknowledge who you are speaking to), *"Hallowed be Your name"* (praise, worship Him). Now notice the very first requests He is asking us to make to God in prayers in the order of prayers: *"Your Kingdom come. "Your will be done on earth as it is in heaven."*

As I said in the previous chapter, Jesus asks us to pray first and foremost that the kingdom of God and His will be done on earth as it is in heaven. What does this mean? Well, I tell you the truth, in heaven, every knee bows and every tongue confesses Jesus as Lord. It is not so on earth.

That's God's mission statement on earth. That everyone will come under His dominion and authority. That's why Paul, writing to Timothy, reveals through the Holy Spirit that God desires that ALL men be saved and come to the knowledge of the truth.

And that's why Jesus reinforced in the same chapter of Mathew 6 that His believers "should seek first the kingdom of God and His righteousness and all other things shall be added unto you".

Therefore, if the gathering of the saints or a church should be a house of prayers, then the overall divine expectation for any gathering of the saints on earth is kingdom expansion. And confession is the evidence of this in the realm of the spirit.

Let me give you four other different practical and real-life scenarios that underscore why it's now important for a shift in focus to proper confession:

Scenario 1 – Confession deemed important, but abused

You would have noticed some Christian denominations in which confession has become the doctrinal pillar. This is good. However, in this case, confession must be made privately in front of a priest.

I suspect this may have been a misapplication of James 5:16: *"Confess your trespasses to one another, and pray for one another, that you may be healed. The effective, fervent prayer of a righteous man avails much."*

Trespass is often translated as sin or fault. In any case, what James is saying here is that for your prayer of healing to be effective, you need to bring to the attention of those who have wronged you their fault, sin or trespasses towards you and ensure forgiveness if you have hurt against anyone.

Yes, every priest, preacher or pastor must make it a habit to bring people to confession especially after the gospel has been preached as the Lord is reemphasizing through this book.

But confession doesn't have to be made in front of the priest unless the priest has wronged you and you want to bring his fault to them to kick off a forgiveness process.

Another erroneous notion of confession in this category is that confession is all you need. This is wrong. That's why you see people go to the priest to confess they have committed murder, stolen or committed sexual sin, again and again. They have the orientation that all you need is confess each time you sin and you are good to go. Well, not quite.

True, confession is so powerful that it doesn't matter how many times you do it, God forgives each time. The angels record your confession as your sins are blotted out of their record book. God said I will remember your sins no more. But each time you commit a new sin, you have given Him something new to remember even though you are still His child.

Don't abuse the power of confession. Imagine if after you just commit a sin and in between the time this happens and when you make confession, you die, losing the opportunity to confess. Dying in sin disqualifies anyone from entering paradise and later, the Kingdom of God.

Imagine that in between the time you commit sin and when you make confession, Jesus appears in the sky with a loud shout, with the voice of the archangel and with the trumpet call of God, for the final flight of His saints. What would be your fate if this happens?

We do not cease to be children of God because we sin after becoming born again when we made the first confession.

But going back to sin simply because grace and confession is available is indicative of misunderstanding of what confession should entail – repentance.

Repentance during confession is accepting that we are dead to sin, no longer a slave to it and turning away from it unto Jesus. We confess Jesus is now Lord over us in repentance. And if this is the case, sin should no longer be Lord, but Jesus. As the Lord, we obey and follow Him as slaves of His righteousness. With the power of the Holy Spirit, we can overcome the temptation to sin.

And if after all is done, we occasionally sin, we do not cease to be children of the Heavenly Father. We confess immediately and ask for His forgiveness. And we are forgiven:

> *"There is therefore now no condemnation to those who are in Christ Jesus, who do not walk according to the flesh, but according to the Spirit.*
>
> *For the law of the Spirit of life in Christ Jesus has made me free from the law of sin and death" (Romans 8:1-2).*

But here, watch what the apostle Paul writes about this:

> *What shall we say then? Shall we continue in sin that grace may abound? Certainly not! How shall we who died to sin live any longer in it?*

Or do you not know that as many of us as were baptized into Christ Jesus were baptized into His death? Therefore we were buried with Him through baptism into death

that just as Christ was raised from the dead by the glory of the Father even so we also should walk in newness of life. (Romans 6:1-4)

Scenario 2- Confession not seen as powerful enough for salvation

The word "preach" means to be a herald, to proclaim or announce something that has been done, for example, in a herald, to publish openly something that was done, for example, on the news media, social media, Facebook etc.

Jesus and the apostles used the word in light of the need to proclaim the gospel – the Kingdom of God and Jesus, the way to it.

Watch this: Jesus was careful in the choice of words when he gave the command for the Great Commission. He understood that the Pharisees and Sadducees did target teaching of the law in enclosed areas.

He did not want His disciples to do the same in respect of the gospel. The gospel needed to be proclaimed as news, run on the rooftops as a herald, scattered on the public field as a seed trusted by the faithful farmer who also trusts heaven for rain and the eventual harvest.

Therefore, He says go into all the world and ``preach``, proclaim as a herald, publish the gospel.

When I see fellow followers of Jesus doing this as street preachers, I am convinced we are doing exactly what Jesus intended when He uttered those words.

But that's not enough. Doing The Great Commission is more than just preaching. Preaching is the first step in a series of work in carrying out this assignment.

In other scriptures, Jesus instructed that in addition to preaching the kingdom of God, to make disciples, baptize and teach them, heal the sick, raise the dead etc. (Mark 16:15, Luke 14:23, Mathew 28:19-20, Acts 1:7-8, Mathew 10:7-11).

One person may not be able to carry out all of these assignment at once. But we need to have this big picture assignment in mind while we solve our own piece of the puzzle at a time.

A preaching engagement that pursues confession or wets the ground for confession is needed before other steps in The Great Commission described in the scripture above.

Let me share with you something that amazed me while preaching on the street. I shared the Good News of the Kingdom of God with two individuals and led them to confession. They confessed their sins and confessed Jesus as Lord over them. We exchanged phone numbers and other contacts.

I gave their contact to a fellow street preacher who was standing by while these people made confession, so that we can both follow up with the new converts.

The third day, I received a text message from my fellow street preacher. He cautioned me never to assume that those converts were saved just because they confessed.

This baffled me, more because it alerted me to another unhelpful attitude towards confession different from the one I describe in scenario 1.

Of course I made out time to engage my fellow preacher and explain to him that confession is that simple and that powerful. It is the evidence that a person has believed in the gospel of the kingdom and has decided to repent.

If there is anything Satan would try as much as possible to do, is to prevent someone from confessing. I recall another instance where I was sharing the gospel with two Canadian soldiers in uniform.

The soldiers had come to have a night out on Whyte Avenue around the time of the Army Remembrance Day in November. After sharing the gospel with them, the Holy Spirit impressed on me they were ready to be invited to receive Jesus.

I told them I was going to lead them to pray for confession. They agreed. Just before I started, a self-proclaimed Satanist, known to most of the street preachers as an adversary of the gospel, cut in to interrupt. He diverted the attention of the soldiers to himself. I asked him to leave, he refused.

He got them into a bet. He told them he could do 60 one-arm pushups for them for $20. Being soldiers who do physical exercise as a daily routine, they were curious to see how this man would accomplish a tedious task even by their own standard.

Then the Satanist moved close to them and whispered into their ears. I assume he told them not to listen to me or perhaps that if he did the 60 pushups with one arm, that`s a good reason they need not listen to me.

Notwithstanding what the Satanist may have whispered to them, the soldiers watched in amazement as the Satanist completes 60 push-ups with one arm.

When he was done, he was neither panting nor sweating. One of the soldiers said to the other: ``how did he do that? It looked so unreal``. ``Yes, it is unreal. It is magic``, I cut in. ``No, he did it because he trained for it``.

The other soldier retorted. That was the end of our conversations as the soldiers hurried back into the bar. So the Satanist prevented them from making the confession.

This he and other Satanists do in several other instances when they notice the preachers are talking to individuals and about to get their listeners to respond.

They are Satan's evangelists sent with a mission to oppose the gospel wherever it's being preached on the streets. I felt a deep sense of loss and a righteous anger that night.

The Lord later reminded me that that was the same way Paul felt when he said Alexander the coppersmith did him a great harm. For the coppersmith resisted the gospel.

Paul in his anger said the Lord will repay Alexander for his works. In previous scriptures, he even said he delivered him to Satan for his evil. The Satanist on Whyte Avenue is the Alexander the coppersmith that opposed Paul in the bible.

In the past, the Satanist had brought a motion before the city council to prohibit street preaching because, according to him, the megaphone results in noise pollution and disturbance to surrounding businesses.

Anyone familiar with Whyte Avenue in Edmonton city would know the farcical angle to the Satanist's claim. With the blast of varied music blaring out of different club bars, the screeching tires and roars from the exhaust of power bikes and many vehicles and the eclectic sounds without a symphony, from street singers hoping for a dime for a living through the night

Whyte Avenue is effectively a place of noise and the sound from a gospel megaphone is often swallowed up by the noise. The Satanist was not concerned for noise to surrounding businesses.

He was carrying out the bidding of his master, Lucifer. Just the same way Alexander, his biblical counterpart, pretended to be defending the interest of businesses and warned that Paul's preaching was a threat to their businesses as relinquishing of idols meant that the people would no longer patronize the coppersmith.

In any case, the Satanist lost the motion and the street preachers were allowed to exercise our right. But as Satan appears to be threatened by the power of confession, the Satanists have not relented in opposing the gospel especially where a confession is about to take place. This is because confession is the real deal when it comes to territorial expansion between God and Satan.

Scenario 3 – Unsaved Leaving a Place for Confession

In a church where I served, we were done Sunday service and it was time for after service reception where members and visitors gathered at the back porch for a meal and drink. I went round to greet and welcome the visitors.

I asked one of the visitors if he was born again. He told me he was an atheist or an agnostic. He said he had come to church as a courtesy to his friend's invitation and that all he heard during the service was good and motivational, inspirational. He doesn't believe in any God and He is indifferent to the whole idea.

In short, he said he was an atheist. "How can anyone come into the house of God, eat consecrated food and still remain an atheist" I jokingly mused to myself. I imagine that an unsaved soul that comes to a church is like someone who had been held for many years by kidnappers.

In the middle of their captivity, they manage to escape to a police station. But the police station is locked or officers are too busy receiving marching orders for the day's duty to notice the person desperately in need of freedom.

At last, the person's chance at freedom is lost and they are recaptured into captivity. As described in the previous chapter, I also imagine an unsaved soul as a little child caught in the middle of a house fire, with no capacity for escape. At the door of the house on fire is a firefighter who needs to break the door open to rescue the little child from fire.

That firefighter is the believer that has a chance to rescue precious souls from the coming fire. And the church a sinner comes to is the fire station. So I said to this my atheist friend visiting the church that morning that I needed to sit with him and have some conversations together. I was determined for a confession. No, I didn't put a gun to his head to get a confession.

Not by might not by power, but by My Spirit says the Lord. The atheist confessed. He got born again right there. And he is today growing in faith. When he moved from the city to British Columbia, he had to rely on me to choose a church for him.

What am saying is that our churches need to be deliberate in inviting people to confession. As believers, we need to be deliberate in inviting people to receive Jesus. Jesus was deliberate in approaching the dreadful Calvary Cross.

Let me give two anecdotes to demonstrate why it's important to be deliberate in getting people to take affirmative actions towards confession. After Sunday service, we exited the sanctuary and I was just about to head home. I spotted the usual display of Christian books by the side.

Behind the display table was seated one of the elders of my church. I took a quick peek at the books without touching anyone of them and I was about to leave. The mama called me back, holding out a book on communion, "this is good", "this is very good", She said.

I imagined that perhaps she knew the author and she was not letting go of me without getting a sale for the author. Communion as a subject didn't interest me as I already considered it important and I cherished it. I didn't think there may be more to know about communion. I am not a very big reader.

And buying a book on communion was certainly the last thing I wanted to do at that point. As though the old woman could read my hesitation and the wonderings of my mind, and like David says, "taste and see that the Lord is good", she persisted in an unyielding salesmanship. "Young man, I have read the book. It is very good. I think you need it and should have it".

She was not concerned if this would upset me because of our cultural differences. She wasn't trying to be politically correct. All she knew was that she had read the book and was convinced every Christian should read it to better appreciate communion and for their own good.

I yielded to her unyielding salesmanship and bought the book. She sounded like a mother. And I said to her in passing that she was like my mother in getting me to buy the book.

She offered to be my spiritual mom, saying that she had even seen me in picture message from the Holy Spirit when she responded in prayers for me.

The atheist confessed. He got born again right there. And he is today growing in faith. When he moved from the city to British Columbia, he had to rely on me to choose a church for him.

From there, a relationship started with her. After I have read the book, a renewed relationship started with communion. The reason is because someone was deliberate in presenting what they have experienced to others and demanding action from them in response. That is the way the gospel of the kingdom ought to be approached.

After it is preached, there needs to be a deliberate invitation to confession. It is our job to make invitation to confession. It is the job of the Holy Spirit to aid in the acceptance of the invitation.

The Holy Spirit has a default disposition: it is to see people come to the kingdom of God through the spread of this good news and invitation to confession. Sometimes the lost may not be ready enough for confession. Unless the Holy Spirit instructs otherwise in specific situations, He expects us to invite to confession and He expects the sinner to make confession.

> *Unless the Holy Spirit instructs otherwise in specific situations, He wants us to invite to confession and He expects the sinner to make confession.*

After preaching the gospel to the crowd at Pentecost, Peter invited the crowd to repent and about three thousand people believed. Secondly, I had just come out of my office to buy some snacks at McDonald restaurant.

I placed my order for the meal I was familiar with and was so eager to have at that moment. After placing my order, the attendant pointed my direction to something else I should instead eat.

She said it was good that I should try it. I wondered whether this was part of their sales policy. Whatever it was, at her insistence, I changed my order and again yielded to a deliberate act of salesmanship.

What am saying here is that we need to be deliberate in presenting the gospel. After presenting the gospel, we need to be deliberate in inviting listeners to take affirmative action in confession.

Kindness Theology

That reminds me of a line of thought that is painfully espoused among many believers today. They claim that all you need is to show your light to the world in good deeds. I call it kindness theology. "As a Christian, you just need to be kind, and people will see your light and come to know Jesus", they say.

Well, our good deeds or kindness should open the door for us to reach the lost. But it is the preaching of the gospel and a response to it in confessionary repentance that saves them. I recall another sad scenario of a Hindu man who is now in his 4o's.

The man's life has been exceptionally touched by kindness to the point he references this every now and then even after the Christian priest, the source of the kindness has passed away. The priest was the principal of the school this man attended in India as a kid.

The man said to me that sometimes he takes his kids to catholic mass just because of the man to learn kindness and good deeds. Then I asked him, "you must be a Christian then, you must be born again"?

He appeared shocked that I imagined him to be a Christian because of his story. He said "oh no. I don't believe in those kind of things. I am a Hindu. We have our own religion".

I applaud the priest because his kind deeds have had much profound impact on the man's life even after decades. But I believe our kindness should always lead people to believe the kind Savior Jesus that we believe.

We should be expressing kindness to the world on His behalf. All our good deeds should be seen by others as coming from Jesus.

Notice what Jesus says, that is often being misinterpreted where emphasis on good deeds unwittingly deemphasizes the need to preach the gospel:

> *"You are the light of the world. A city that is set on a hill cannot be hidden. Nor do they light a lamp and put it under a*

> *basket, but on a lamp stand, and it gives light to all who are in the house. Let your*

> *light so shine before men, that they may see your good works and glorify your Father in heaven." (Mathew 5:14-16)*

Let's break this down one by one. First, Jesus is the light of the world as John the Beloved records. Knowing that He will be leaving the world and His disciples will be living in Him and He in them, He says they are now the light of the world.

Letting your light shine means you let Jesus shine, be seen, be known in your good deeds or acts of kindness. And Jesus says that when others see your good deeds, they should glorify your Father in heaven.

To take you through God's justice system so you can be discharged, acquitted and free, Jesus needs your admittance to the sin-crime committed

First, Jesus said this because He doesn't want them to behave like the Pharisees and Sadducees who liked to show off and receive praise for their good deeds.

Second, I believe by the time people glorify your father in heaven because of your good deeds, they now know Jesus. They now worship Jesus. They now believe in Jesus. Having the lost confessing they have sinned and confessing that Jesus paid for their sins with His blood should be the goal of every good deed from a believer to a non-believer.

Scenario 4- Confession in the Criminal Justice System

Many of today's modern and valued professions have their foundations influenced by biblical doctrines, teachings and practices. For the legal profession, confessions were first developed by the Roman Catholic Church. Today, the criminal justice system uses confession from an accused person to establish guilt.

The law is generally in favor of cross-checking confession by the accused person with other pieces of evidence like exhibits, testimonies from other witnesses and an established fact to show that confession was not obtained from the accused by force or when they are deemed not mentally fit.

But overall, confession is usually considered as the best piece of evidence of a crime in the justice system. The same is with God's spiritual law regarding confession. The bible says that all of mankind have sinned and have come short of the glory of God.

The sentencing for the sin-crime is eternal death. But the gift of God is eternal life through Jesus Christ. In God's criminal justice system, Jesus is the only defense attorney. He qualified for this position because He shed His blood on Calvary Cross for all the sin-crimes committed by humankind.

To take you through God's justice system so you can be discharged, acquitted and free, Jesus needs your admittance to the sin-crime committed. He needs your guilty plea. He needs your confession to create a glorified body for you when He shows up for the final flight of the saints.

Here is one other insight regarding a sinner's genuine confession – it is a legal statement to which God is bound.

In God's spiritual law court, whenever an argument is made using the blood of Jesus, a strong and the only legitimate case for the acquittal of the sinner-criminal has been made. And it would be a miscarriage of justice for God to ignore or turn down the request for acquittal.

God loves justice. In fact, the psalmist says repeatedly, *"righteousness and justice are the foundations of His throne."(Psalm 89:14, 97:2).* That is what John the beloved apostle had in mind when he said *"If we confess our sins, He is faithful and "just" to forgive us our sins and to cleanse us from all unrighteousness." (1 John 1:9).*

He is faithful to His word of promise that He will always hear our prayers of confession and will forgive. He is "just" because He Himself set up the justice system in which only through the blood of Jesus there can be forgiveness.

CHAPTER 17– THE LAST REVIVAL

It was a Sunday afternoon at about 2:15pm on May 19, 2013. I was just about driving into the compound for a service at a church where I was helping out.

The day before, I had just been walked out by security guards from the Southgate Mall in Edmonton city while sharing the gospel message with people inside the shopping mall.

As I was driving on that Sunday afternoon, I was filled with intense concern for the people of Canada, that many people have rejected God. I was quite worried, knowing the fate of anyone who does not have Jesus in their life. I was worried for the unavoidable consequence of rejecting Jesus.

I was particularly concerned that society is shutting its doors to anything God, Christian, Jesus, gospel, given my experience the previous day. I was almost too overwhelmed by the thoughts and my concern.

At that point, God said to me somehow audibly to the point I looked back in the car to see if someone else was sitting behind. Here is what Jesus said to me:

> *"Joshua, why are you getting walked up on this? A time is coming and is very soon.*

People will be rushing to church without being invited, begging for repentance. It will be like the days of John the Baptist."

On hearing this, I looked around the car again. I was comforted by the word as I thought this meant there will be revival again.

At the same time, it triggered a different set of concern and curiosity. I trusted every bit of the word from the Lord. But I was curious to know what would make people to rush to church without being invited and in this case, they will be coming to beg for repentance, not blessing, deliverance or healing.

"Could a major disaster be a cause for this?" I pondered on it as I entered the church. I was asked to lead intercessory prayers in church. When I got back to my seat after leading the prayers, a fairly elderly prophetess approached me.

She said "Brother Joshua, the Lord gave you a word today. Why didn't you share it while on the pulpit?" It was quite shocking to me. At the same time I felt that was how God is deciding to confirm His word to me.

I told the prophetess that I didn't know I was meant to share it on the pulpit as I was only asked to lead intercessory prayers.

At a later service, I shared the word when I had the opportunity. For several weeks and months, I inquired of the Lord for further answers to my curiosities regarding the word.

About 2 years later, I received a message on WhatsApp messaging app. It was a message regarding a vision circulated and was purported to have been written by a well-known African preacher.

It was later confirmed that the African preacher did not write the message. It was also assumed that whoever wrote the message saw the vision but used the name of the African preacher to spread the message of the vision.

Whatever the case may be, when I saw the message, it was impressed on me by the Holy Spirit that that was the answer to my curiosity regarding the word I had received in 2013.

The fellow had been in a dream-vision that happened to them twice. They saw a crowd of people running to different churches calling for repentance. According to this fellow, it was as if a spirit of dread had fallen on the people running to church.

It was made clear to him in the vision that the final flight had just happened and the antichrist has taken over the reign of the world as a one-world government.

The people running to church remember what the Christians had preached in the past and they were quickly able to see that the believers were right. And some of them were believers who were not prepared for the flight. It is the last revival. They will run to church without being asked to. They will run to beg for repentance and there will be no answer.

The faithful believers of Jesus will have been taken away from the earth by Jesus.

Those left behind will be subject to untold suffering never experienced in the history of mankind under the seven years of the global reign of the antichrist in the Great Tribulation.

During this time, only those who agree to be tattooed with the mark of the beast (the antichrist) will be able to buy, sell, and access essential services of life.

Once they have the mark of the beast, Satan has a legal hold on their eternal destiny in the Lake of Fire. Only a few people, some of those who understood what the bible says, and the consequence of the mark will be able to painstakingly resist the mark. Angels and the two witnesses described in revelation will be deployed to preach a gospel that warns people to repent because of the judgment ahead.

The Antichrist will begin his reign with deception as the man of peace and he will deceive many into believing that he is the Messiah expected by the Jewish people. Unfortunately, many of those left behind will fall for his deception and others in stark defiance to God, will obtain the mark of the antichrist and will be forever sealed with Satan.

When Jesus comes a second time, the few people who are painstaking in the Great Tribulation and are obedient to God, will have a chance again. That's why I have always believed and expressed a concern for others that don't yet have a relationship with Jesus. The concern is that right now, grace for redemption is like an ocean. When Jesus takes away His believers in the final flight, grace will be a drop in the same ocean.

CHAPTER 18 – A GLORIOUS JOURNEY

It first began with Adam and Eve. God visited with them in the beautiful Garden of Eden on earth. They also visited with God in the heavenly Kingdom (the 4th heaven) and were escorted by angels back and forth Eden.

God began to physically demonstrate the flight of humans that defy gravity from the righteous Enoch, who was taken up. This demonstration of the final flight journey continued with Elijah the prophet. He was taken up in a chariot of fire after his mission on earth.

Jesus continued this demonstration in the New Testament after he rose from the dead during his departure from the earth and He ascended to heaven with His glorified body.

God used this to show that at the coming of Jesus for the final journey of His believers from the earth, the dead in Christ, the righteous dead will be the first to rise to meet Jesus in the air.

And those who are alive at His coming will be taken up like Enoch, Elijah and Jesus. Jesus had to ascend to heaven with His glorified body.

At the coming of Jesus who will trigger the resurrection of the righteous dead, everyone embarking on the journey with Him to heaven will need a glorified body.

Eden is a spiritual existence on the earth. No human geography has been able to pin-point its location on earth because it is indeed a spiritual existence on the earth. The four heads of river flowing out of Eden that are described by Moses indicate that bodies of water surround this beautiful garden.

This reinforces my conclusion in this book that Eden is paradise. Remember that in the open vision I had to the border of paradise, I describe that from what seemed like a mighty rock on which I was standing, I could see below it a vast expanse of river, crystal clear like glass.

After the fall into sin, Adam and Eve were driven out of the garden and a superior angel was installed by God to guard the Garden, according to the book of Genesis.

I have let you know in this book that paradise, the third heaven, or Abraham's bosom as Jesus also calls it, referenced severally in the scriptures, is the once deserted Garden of Eden. It is now occupied by all the redeemed saints, born again, "taken away" righteous people of God.

Paradise or Eden is now occupied by righteous people including righteous Abel to Noah, Enoch, Abraham, Isaac, Jacob, the 12 patriarchs, to Moses and Elijah, David and the righteous kings, to the New Testament righteous people.

These include John the Baptist and apostles of Jesus, Peter, James, John, Paul and other early church believers of Jesus to all the saints who have departed the earth in this church age. They are all residents of God's paradise.

Jesus visits with them and they are often escorted by the angels to visit with Jesus in the 4th heaven, the heavenly kingdom.

They all got to paradise through faith, obedience, righteous deeds, sacrifices to God, and the new birth experience simply because God accepts the blood of Jesus the Lamb of God who was slain from the foundation of the world, for the remission of sins for all of humanity.

In the open vision in November 2016, which I recounted to you in chapter 1, which was repeated again in February 2017, I also got to the border of paradise. Escorted by Jesus, I crossed the river like a sea of glass and was standing on a huge mountain.

Like many accounts of the bible foreshadowing things in the future, the exodus of Israel nation from Egypt foreshadowed what God intends to do in the final flight

On the other side of where I was standing penetrated the most beautiful thing I had ever heard. It was the song of worship, classical, angelic, and human blended together. I disengaged from the experience when it was interrupted.

Just before that, I knew someone would have to come get me to the place the songs were coming from as there was a huge gap between the mountain I was standing and where the residents of paradise were.

These residents of God's transitional heaven live adjacent to Hades or hell, the temporary abode of Satan and his demons and all the departed disobedient who will be eventually cast into the Lake of Fire at the end.

Not only do the residents of God's paradise currently enjoy unexplainable bliss in the presence of Jesus, still unlike their Hades counterpart, there is a solid hope they so eagerly wait for. It is the descending and appearance of Jesus in the sky happening very soon as Paul wrote to the Thessalonian church.

It is the appearance of Jesus Himself with a loud shout. It is the appearance of Jesus with the voice of the archangel. It is the appearance of Jesus with the trumpet call of God. Their hope is Jesus' declaration of victory over death with His loud shout.

Their hope is Jesus' creation of resurrection, glorified body for everyone traveling with Him through the voice of the Seraph, the archangel.

Their hope is the final trumpet of God setting the travel in motion. Though residents of paradise are currently in abundant joy, peace, love, they are eagerly waiting for their glorified body, on the glorious day of the Lord, to a glorious journey, into a glorious destination – the Heavenly Kingdom of God.

Here they will be treated as bride by the Husband of the church at the great wedding banquet – the marriage supper of the Lamb. So paradise residents are eager for that fateful final flight to the Kingdom of God where they will be with the Lord forever.

Why shouldn't you and I be expectant of this journey like the departed righteous in paradise? The scripture says, after the dead in Christ have risen to meet Jesus in the air for the flight,

> *"[...] Then we who are alive and remain shall be caught up together with them in the*

> *clouds to meet the Lord in the air. And thus we shall always be with the Lord (1 Thessalonians 4:17).*

During this glorious journey to the kingdom of God in which we fly in our glorified body with Jesus, we will be too lost for words at God's awesomeness, His majesty and omnipotence.

Imagine travelling on the same journey with many saints of old, as old as the righteous Abel in Genesis, to Noah, Abraham, Isaac and Jacob.

Imagine the humble but great Moses. Imagine Joshua the mighty man of valor. Imagine Elijah. Imagine the New Testament apostles and disciples. Though all in our glorified bodies, imagine you eventually see what Peter, James and John look like. Imagine the Apostle Paul, John the Beloved.

As for me, I am so eager to see what Paul, Peter and Jonah look like because of their amusing character. I also want to see Brother Eutychus, who was sleeping on the window of a skyscraper and fell to his death while Paul was preaching the longest sermon ever preached. Thankfully, he was raised to life. I hope the seven sons of Sceva eventually made it to paradise and I will see them during this journey.

The bible records that they were beaten and ran away naked by the demons they were trying to cast out. I hope you know I do not intend to poke fun at them during the flight!

Please, send me an email or connect to the dedicated website for this book and the subject. Let me know which bible character you long to see during this flight and why. Again, I couldn't resist the temptation for a lighter mood on this crucial subject. Let's continue with the journey.

You have only read about these characters in the bible. But now they are travelling along with you. History comes alive with historical artifacts. In this case, history is resurrected, with eyes to see, ears to hear, mouth to speak and skin to touch. Imagine travelling along with billions of righteous people and the angels of God in a suspended roller coaster that is just you.

Imagine the feeling that you have just been delivered from the slavery of this world full of sickness, diseases, death, discomfort, violence and homelessness.

Imagine the thought that you have just escaped the reign of the antichrist in the world and The Great Tribulation. Imagine looking forward to the glorious destination in the heavenly kingdom and endlessly being dazzled and amazed at surprises that God had for you.

That's why the bible says "[...*eye has not seen, nor ear heard, nor have entered into the heart of man the things which God has prepared for those who love him*" *(1 Corinthians 2:9)*. Our imagination is too limited to grasp what God has prepared for us in His kingdom, starting from the journey to it.

Like many accounts of the bible foreshadowing things in the future, the exodus of Israel nation from Egypt foreshadowed what God intends to do in the final flight.

God's pillar of cloud by day and pillar of fire by night shielded the nation of Israel from every harm the Egyptians or the dangerous terrain of the wilderness could have inflicted on them.

God was using this to demonstrate His awesomeness, power and majesty over every terrain no matter how obscure it could be. He got 600,000 men to travel through the wilderness and the Red Sea all at once. It was an estimated 1-2.5 million people including women and children.

There was no report of an accident on the way. There was no report of a wild beast attack. They travelled in safety, peace, provision and joy as they had enjoyed safety in Goshen when the Egyptians were in deep mourning as a result of the 10 plagues.

In the same way, paradise is like Goshen for the righteous dead in the heavens who live adjacent to hell (Egypt), which is the inner extension of Satan's command and control Centre in the kingdom of the air (Pharaoh's throne). The righteous lived in safety and peace in paradise.

Now pay attention to this. The righteous dead were held in this temporary waiting heavenly place (paradise) for as long as humanity has existed.

This is because God wants to do exactly the same thing He did when He moved all His people at once away from

Egypt through the dangerous wilderness with animal and human enemies on the way.

He did this to demonstrate His awesome power over a dangerous situation and terrain.

Jesus will bring *"other sheep that are not of this fold"* (the Old Testament righteous dead living in paradise) together with this flock, (the living righteous on earth), so *there will be one flock* (John 10:16) at the final flight.

So God will use this one flock of billions of righteous saints from the creation of mankind to demonstrate His awesomeness again as they journey without harm through the dangerous terrain of the kingdom of the air into the kingdom of God.

The power of Satan and his warring princes in the air will be suspended as they watch the parade of the saints. In just the same way the pillar of cloud by day and the pillar of fire by night caused a suspension of the power of the Egyptian enemies.

In just the same way there was a suspension of the power of the enemy when the 400 prophets of Baal could not cause Baal to manifest because God wanted to demonstrate His power through Elijah who called down fire to consume the sacrifice.

In just the same way Daniel was thrown into the lions' den and the lions were muted and unable to even roar at him because God was with him. The final flight with Jesus is one big thing God Himself is waiting for because He wants to demonstrate His omnipotence to His enemies and His awesomeness to His righteous people.

His people will journey through the kingdom of the air. They will see the enemy. But the enemy's power will be too suspended for them to interrupt the journey. I can only imagine the spectacle of shame God wanted to subject Satan His enemy to, using this event.

I tried to laugh in Russian when I imagined the extent of disgrace Satan and his fallen princes will experience at this moment during the journey. We will be filled with awe of God, Jesus the King of Kings and the Lord of Lords and His Holy angels. One more thing will happen to us as it did happen to biblical Israel.

I remember God telling me that 2016 was a year of "Burst into Songs". And I can tell you that in that year I received several songs from the Holy Spirit that I sang from my dreams to the time I woke up. They were songs I had never heard before. And I am not gifted with music or a singing voice.

But watch this, something happened to biblical Israel nation. Yes, God delivered them from 430 years of slavery that Passover night when they left Egypt.

God caused their Egyptian enemies to be favorable to them, hence the Egyptians handed their treasury- articles of gold and silver to the fleeing nation of Israel and Israel became wealthy overnight to grow a brand new economy for 600, 000 people (excluding women and children).

Israel was hurried out of Egypt. They were pursued by the Egyptian warlords as they journeyed through the wilderness.

So they never had a moment to pause, rest, and digest what their eyes had just seen regarding their freedom from slavery and how God spared them in Goshen from the ten plagues in Egypt.

They were still in awe of the pillar of cloud by day and pillar of fire by night that visibly demonstrated the presence of God with them. No sign for celebration or a cause for it yet as the Egyptians were still in pursuit. But when they crossed the red sea and noticed that their Egyptian slave masters have drowned in the same sea, they had just crossed the Rubicon.

The bridge with slavery was now burned behind them. It was the first time freedom became very real to them. And the Promised Land was within reach.

They now had the time to process in their mind all of these things that God has done for them. They were too lost for words. They could do nothing else other than to burst into songs spontaneously.

With tears of joy, they worshipped and praised the living God for His awesomeness with songs they had never learned before.

All of a sudden, they became music composers. Suddenly, a people, including their leaders, Moses and Miriam, with no records of singing or composing songs whether in the bible or in historical books, reached an emotional peak.

They did the unthinkable. They burst into a song that describes what they saw God do, (Exodus 15). The song was composed, choreographed and sang almost at the same time.

Even though they were not talented singers nor had they any experience with singing, by the time they will finish singing, they have composed a new song. 600,000 people without microphones sang in harmony in worship, adoration and praise to the Most High God.

It was a spark of the divine! It was spontaneous! It was simultaneous! It was my experience when I visited the border of paradise as described at the beginning of this book. On reaching the top of the mountain close to the border of paradise, I burst into tears with spontaneous singing.

And the brethren in church service on the earth with me on that Friday night joined in the singing because it was a familiar song. And after that night experience, none of us remembered the song that we sang when it happened. The same thing happened in the dream-vision with Jesus on the same flight. Having been overwhelmed with the warmth of Jesus in the sea, I burst into spontaneous worship to Him.

During the final flight with Jesus, the spark of the divine will come in again. The loud shout will be heard from Jesus. The voice of the archangel, a seraph, will bring forth the confession or salvation prayers of the saints to create their glorified body.

And once the trumpet call of God is sounded, the travel is set in motion. The righteous dead in paradise will receive their glorified body, defy gravity and march out to meet Jesus in the air.

The living righteous on the earth will receive their glorified body and also be enabled to fly to meet others in the air with Jesus, exactly the way the scripture describes it and based on what Jesus showed me through the open vision, which was repeated in a dream-vision.

On the way, Jesus will be showing us the rivers Moses describes in the book of Genesis that flow from Eden. The thrill and excitement from this flight experience will by no way compare to the earthly cruise ship experience.

The cruise ship thrill is often stifled by the concern that we will soon return to life as usual. In this case, we will be looking forward to a buildup of the excitement as God will continue to whao us with His awesomeness through the journey and for eternity.

I have a feeling that though some residents of paradise have had escorted visits to the kingdom of God, God has not revealed the location of these rivers to them yet or they have not been allowed the experience of travelling through them, so we all have equal moments of surprise. We will experience these spiritual rivers in just the same way Israel experienced walking on dry land in the middle of the deep red sea.

The bible says that the secret things belong to God. Those He reveals belongs to us and our children forever (Deuteronomy 29:29). I journeyed with Jesus to the border of paradise twice through a river in which I even saw the sea bed and I was warm.

Israel journeyed through the red sea without getting wet or drowned. In the same way, we will journey through the rivers surrounding Eden that Moses describes in the book of Genesis during the final flight with Jesus. After crossing the rivers, we can expect to burst into songs like Israel did.

Like Israel did, we will burst into tears of joy with songs never before learned or choreographed. Our experience will invoke the spark of the divine to effect this

As the fulfillment of the promised heavenly land in the Kingdom of God is within grasp, the angelic voices with beautiful music in worship to God will bring the air of the gates of heaven.

The righteous dead traveling from paradise will be used to the angels worshipping with them while they were in the waiting area in paradise.

The living righteous traveling from the earth will have been prepared by their experience of worship which will increase shortly before the coming of Jesus. Every travelling companion of Jesus will be sparked by the divine to burst into songs.

As the gospel of the kingdom will be preached to every nation before Jesus comes for the final flight, you can expect people from every nation, race, ethnicity, tribe and generation to be singing along.

As Israel composed a brand new song and sang spontaneously by the spark of the divine, all the travelers will be enabled by the same spark to compose, choreograph and sing a brand new song describing their experience of the awesomeness of God and His deliverance.

We will continue singing until we get to the Promised Land in the kingdom of God (the 4th heaven). Here we will be welcomed by a great banquet known as the marriage supper of the Lamb, prepared by Jesus. And we will forever be with the Lord.

If this were a movie, your anticipation to see it should be higher than the roof. If you were to be a cast in the movie, your excitement for this should be beyond measure. But guess what? It is not a movie, nor a mere fantasy. It is a promise by a reputable promise keeper. Jesus never for once lied.

Not one of His words in the bible has failed to be fulfilled and not one will fail. The next big prophetic promise that Jesus made and yet to be fulfilled is His return for the final flight of His saints. And it will happen extremely soon. Jesus showed me this repeatedly.

He showed several other believers some of whom have gone for a visit to heaven and back, including Mary K. Baxter. I encourage you to buy all of her books for yourself and your church. They will equip you spiritually.

Baxter's books will also equip you to be horizontally focused on the command to reach out to the lost and bring them to the kingdom of God.

And if you have not yet repented from sin and been born again, this is the time to do so. The bible says *"If we confess our sins, He is faithful and just to forgive us our sins and to cleanse us from all unrighteousness." (1 John 1:9)*.

The blood Jesus shed on Calvary cross for your redemption is still flowing now. The bible also says that "[…] if you confess with your mouth the Lord Jesus and believe in your heart that God has raised Him from the dead, you will be saved. (Romans 10:9).

Finally, the bible says *"For with the heart one believes unto righteousness, and with the mouth confession is made unto salvation." (Romans 10:10)*.

If you want to repent of sin and receive Jesus as Lord and savior now so you can be ready for the final flight with Him, can you say this prayer. Would you bow down wherever you are now and say this:

> *Father in heaven, according to your word, by the reason of sins that I committed and by the reason of who I am, I confess before you that I have sinned.*
>
> *I confess that I am a sinner. I thank you for sending your son Jesus to shed His blood for the forgiveness of my sins. I believe in the blood of Jesus that is able to wash me clean.*
>
> *I ask for your forgiveness now as I repent from them. Jesus, come into my heart as I make you my personal Lord and Savior. I thank you heavenly Father. In Jesus name I pray. Amen*

If you have made the above prayer, I say congratulations to you. You have just been accepted into God's big family. Find a good church to attend. You can also connect with me whether or not you made this prayer at finalflight@ruwemi.org. I would love to hear your thoughts on what I have shared in this book.

May God bless and keep you till Jesus returns. I pray that God will release revelations to you on this subject directly. I pray that you and I will be passengers in the glorious flight with Jesus. Amen.

*Join the movement to tell the
world that Jesus is coming soon*

CHAPTER 19- A CALL TO ACTION

If this book has blessed you, get a copy online or through the distribution channels on the book's website, for someone else or give them your copy. If you have people that need salvation, get a copy for them. Go tell it on the mountain of Facebook and other social media. Go tell it on the mountain of your church, your home, your office, your school, your country, state, province, city, town and village. Go tell it on the mountain of your street, your market place and entertainment industry.

That Jesus Christ is Lord. That Jesus Christ will soon appear in the sky. That Jesus Christ will take away His believers from the world when He appears. That all the saints of God, dead and alive, will be taken away in The Final Flight to the heavenly kingdom.

That everyone who confesses their sins and receive Jesus as Lord and savior will qualify for The Final Flight. That the time for repentance, redemption and restoration is now. That the next minute might be too late.

Make confession a focal point of your church service. It is Jesus' desire as described earlier and because the essence of the church is kingdom expansion. Teach the believers on the end time prophecies and direct their attention to the soon-to-happen glorious journey and the heavenly destination. Get out of the church walls to preach the gospel to every nation.

The Final Flight Video

We are making a video on The Final Flight, destined for social media. This video will feature real individual believers testifying to the world about the coming of Jesus and the need to accept Him now. A longer version of the video will showcase churches all over the world, with individual church identity, saying the same message of the Final Flight. Join the course at www.thefinalflight.org

The Final Flight Forum and Symposium

The dedicated website for this book and the video mentioned above also contains a forum to which you can contribute messages, revelations and insights you have received regarding the subject of the final flight and that you would like to share for others to see. A yearly symposium will also be planned on this subject.

Weekly Meditation Drills

I want to suggest to you to practice thinking about this subject for once or twice in a week. Take some 20 minutes and relax. Imagine the description of this glorious flight that the Holy Spirit inspired me to write. If you do this consistently, your perspective to life will change. Then prayerfully examine yourself to see if you are ready for the final flight should the boarding process begin. You already know it will begin without prior notice. Remember the parable of the ten virgins, five of whom were not ready in spite of being born again and baptized in the Holy Spirit. I pray for you and myself that this will not be our fate in Jesus name. Amen!

Epilogue

1. Marriage Supper of the Lamb – on reaching their destination in the heavenly kingdom, the saints of Jesus will be treated to an indescribable reception known as the Marriage Supper of the Lamb. You don't want to miss this!

2. The Antichrist Reign – immediately after the exit of believers of Jesus from the earth in the final flight, the Beast, the man of lawlessness, Satan's messenger, known as the Antichrist , will take over the reign of the world in a one-world government.

   He will first deceive those who are left behind as a man of peace. He will then later put himself in place of God. He will institute a reign of horror in what is known as The Great Tribulation. Only those who receive the mark of the beast, his seal of approval will be able to buy or sell.

3. The Great Tribulation – in the reign of the antichrist lasting for seven years in total, anyone who receives the mark of the beast (the antichrist) will enjoy a temporary social benefit for siding with him, but they will be forever condemned with him and Satan in the Lake of Fire.

   Anyone who does not receive the mark will suffer greater horror but will have the last chance for salvation if they believe in Jesus. But this will be extremely difficult, almost impossible to bear the horror of the antichrist without his mark.

Grace for redemption is like an ocean now. Grace for redemption then will be just like a drop in the same ocean. Now is the time of salvation!

4. The Second Coming of Jesus – Jesus will come back to the world to gather the remnant of His believers and the Battle of the Armageddon follows.

5. The Battle of the Armageddon – a final epic and cosmic war between God's angels/people/Jesus and Satan/the antichrist/ Satan's princes /demons/disobedient people.

6. The Millennial Reign of Christ – After the epic and cosmic war of the Armageddon, Jesus Christ will reign on the earth as the king of kings for one thousand years with all His saints. He will bring heaven on earth. The saints of God will be kings and priests.

7. The Great White Throne Judgment – a judgment of rewards in heaven for the saints of God. Some people sometimes think reward will come to believers based on how many people they have won to the kingdom of God. But this is wrong. We will be rewarded based on God's wisdom and the extent of our obedience to God's instruction for the salvation of sinners.

8. The Lake of Fire – at the very end, there is a permanent dwelling place for sinners and Satan who have been living temporarily in Hades (Hell). It is the Lake of Fire.

9. Death and Hell in the Lake of Fire– Death is a spirit. It dwells in Hell from where it goes to the earth to take people's lives. At the end, Death itself and Hell, which according to Jesus' description of it

recorded by Mary Baxter, is like the shape of a human being, will be cast into the Lake of Fire. And there will be no more death for the people of God.

10. A New Heaven and a New Earth – God will destroy the whole earth and heaven, after the Battle of the Armageddon. He will create a New Heaven and a New Earth and He will dwell with humans and His angels forever and ever.

THE END

ABOUT THE AUTHOR

Joshua Adetunji lives in Edmonton, Canada with his wife and two children. He is the founder and president of Rise Up and Walk Evangelistic Ministry International, Edmonton (RUWEMI Ministries). Joshua is passionate about soul-winning and kingdom expansion through a united effort. He has ministered in several ministries. Joshua may be reached at finalflight@ruwemi.org or admin@ruwemi.org. www.ruwemi.org.

RUWEMI Ministries

Made in the USA
Lexington, KY
09 May 2018